A Rainbow Book

Praise for *The Art of Instant Message*—

Dating, and certainly online dating can be intimidating and stress-ful. The challenge to make a connection with someone, build rap-port and eventually meet in person so that you can truly under-stand your compatibility, takes confidence and a well-thought-out process. Keith's advice regarding how to best utilize instant mes-saging is a welcomed addition to the world of online dating and will serve everyone well as they aim to succeed in finding a long-term relationship.

—Michael Egan, CEO of Spark Networks
(owner of JDate.com and ChristianMingle.com)

The *Art* of Instant Message

Be Yourself
Be Confident
Be Successful
Communicating Personality

KEITH GRAFMAN

Rainbow Books, Inc.
FLORIDA

Library of Congress Cataloging-in-Publication Data

Names: Grafman, Keith, 1983- author.
Title: The art of instant message : be yourself, be confident, be successful
  communicating personality / Keith Grafman.
Description: Highland City, FL : Rainbow Books, Inc., [2016]
Identifiers: LCCN 2015036719| ISBN 9781568251820 (perfect trade softcover :
  alk. paper) | ISBN 9781568251837 (epub)
Subjects: LCSH: Online dating. | Instant messaging. | Online etiquette.
Classification: LCC HQ801.82 .G73 2016 | DDC 302.23/11–dc23
LC record available at http://lccn.loc.gov/2015036719

The Art of Instant Message: Be Yourself, Be Confident,
Be Successful Communicating Personality
© 2016 by Keith Grafman

Softcover ISBN 978-1-56825-182-0
EPUB (ebook) ISBN 978-1-56825-183-7

Published by

Rainbow Books, Inc.
P. O. Box 430
Highland City, FL 33846-0430

Editorial Offices and Wholesale/Distributor Orders

Telephone: (863) 648-4420
RBIbooks@aol.com
RainbowBooksInc.com

Author's Blog

AdviceForDaters.com

Individuals' Orders

Toll-free Telephone (800) 431-1579
Amazon.com · AllBookStores.com · BookCH.com · BN.com · Kobo.com

Disclaimer: This book is not intended to serve as a substitute for psychological or relationship advice or counseling. The reader is encouraged to seek professional counseling regarding any problematic communication or relationship issues encountered in the real world of online dating. Although the conversations described are based on actual exchanges, all correspondent names are fictitious and all identifying information has been removed.

Author photograph by Joel Barhamand.

First Edition 2016
19   18   17   16   7 6 5 4 3 2 1
Created, published and printed in the United States of America.

To my parents, Arlene and Les Grafman,
who always had so much wonderful faith in me,
believing that I can accomplish anything.

To my amazing wife, Stephanie . . .
for your unconditional love, support and encouragement.
It was the search for you that made this all possible.
I am so grateful to you and, most of all, that I found you.

Contents

Contents

Preface

For as long as I can remember, finding companionship was one of my goals. I've always felt that making a great connection with people enhances every aspect of life. Ultimately, life is far more fulfilling when there is someone special to share it with.

While I dated in junior high and high school, my experience was naturally very limited, which made it difficult to know what I was looking for in a girlfriend. That, however, was when instant messaging (IM-ing) became very popular and prevalent.

During my junior year of college, around the time Facebook and Myspace were first making a lot of noise, the online dating scene was just beginning to gain popularity, and IM was a commonly used online dating tool. We used instant message (IM) for chat between friends when we were in our dorms.

Most people used IM every day during my college years, and students commonly exchanged IM screen names. I always thought of IM as more of a means to flirt, but since every conversation is private, I realized it would be easy to flirt while relaxing in the dorms or when taking a break from studies.

I felt communicating via IM made flirting easier because it helped me avoid in-person rejection. Even when I would ask a girl out on a date, if she replied "no" via instant message, the rejection seemed infinitely more soft—mainly because no one was there to witness it. If a rejection is done privately, you can, in a sense, carry on as if it didn't happen, thereby being less affected by it.

IM also provides a larger window of time to craft each message with precision, as opposed to a face-to-face discussion, during which extended pauses can become awkward silences. For example, if a friend was nearby when I used IM, I could always ask for advice—the girl would never know what was really happening on my end of the conversation. The same could have been the case on her end, and I would not have known.

My brother was fortunate enough to have met his amazing wife in college, but for those of us who didn't meet the "right one" in a traditional way, dating is more difficult. I dated a number of women I met in the traditional way during college, but none of the relationships materialized beyond six- to seven-month flings. Eventually, I signed up on a few online dating sites; Jdate.com and PlentyOfFish.com were among the first.

Just like most online daters, when I began to use online dating sites, I was ambivalent. I worried that I might get no responses and was concerned I wouldn't find anyone normal or that I would be negatively judged for having used an online dating site. Some people object to online dating because they claim it isn't an "organic" way to meet, but I disagree. Of course, the most organic way to meet, in my opinion, is through a group of friends. But aside from meeting your soulmate in school or being introduced by a mutual friend, online dating is just as organic as meeting at a bar, club or serendipitously.

When I realized IM was a tool made available at online dating sites, I decided to jump in and hit the ground running. To my delight, the IM skills I had developed in college were very useful. I found instant messaging to be an effective way to project my personality online and a powerful means to quickly establish rapport with potential matches.

That is not to say that e-mail isn't valuable. Many people are not comfortable using IM, especially if they are new to computers or are shy. In some cases, e-mail may be the only way to connect with people who may not want to make themselves available via IM. But even in those circumstances, the skills used for IM are incredibly germane to all online dating communication.

After college, I became close friends with Paul Aviles, who I met while working at an advertising agency in Manhattan. We had two passions in common: music and the quest for companionship. In the realm of dating, Paul always felt comfortable meeting women "on the fly," whereas I always felt it was difficult to create social context that way. I felt it was easier to meet women via online dating sites rather than in a bar. I didn't limit myself to online dating; however, I felt it was much easier to meet people within a controlled environment.

When hanging out in Manhattan with our groups of friends, Paul and I talked with many people about dating—a very common topic, frequently discussed. I often found myself giving guys pep talks about the dating process of using both online communication and in-person formalities. I described successful strategies I'd developed to establish a rapport with my dates.

Paul and I have given each other much great advice over the years. He recognized and continuously praised my ability to create powerful social context and genuine rapport with women online. One day Paul told me I should find a way to teach people my skills. He insisted that there are many people, men and women, who could benefit from my knowledge in their efforts to find companionship.

I thought to myself, *It feels good to help people. Could there be career potential in this?*

Paul suggested I write a book to help teach the communication skills I had developed.

After considering the possibility of writing a book and doing some research, I decided that if I were going to pursue a career as a dating advisor, I would have to make my mark by breaking into the field with a product that didn't already exist. It was then I decided to write *The Art of Instant Message.*

Introduction

This book was written with a sole purpose: to break down the elements of real time, online dating dialog. I help make it easier for you to express genuine personality and be captivating while instant messaging (IM-ing). If you are either new to online dating or have just not been successful in the process, this book may help improve your online dating communications. It will teach you how to take the first step on the path to finding companionship by being yourself.

Developing a personal strategy to project your personality will be an ongoing process. Online daters have good days and bad days. Rejection is inevitable. The goal is to minimize it, and developing a personal strategy will help.

What Is Strategic IM-ing?

Strategic IM-ing is an effective method of adapting personality by transliterating expressiveness and mannerisms while subtly directing the flow of dialog. People generally approach IM dialog as they do text messaging—they use it for casual dialog, passing up an opportunity to make a strong impression. With strategy, IM can be a very powerful communication tool.

When a girl is sitting at her computer, and, of course, if she is willing to make time to chat with you, she's somewhat relaxed. So, in a sense, you're catching her off guard. For example, if she is at work and is about to step into a meeting, she's probably not going to answer your message. But if she isn't busy, she may be relaxed enough to respond. It would be similar to getting a girl's attention while she is sitting on a train; she's unguarded because she isn't anticipating an interaction. This is in contrast to a bar's atmosphere, where girls are often guarded by their friends and expect to be approached. So, when a girl is approached by an online dater who captures her interest, the IM-er has a chance to make a powerful first impression in a relaxed, controlled setting.

What Strategic IM-ing Is Not

I want to emphasize that I am writing this book to help people find genuine companionship. If you bought this book with the hope that it will teach you how to get sex via online dating, then you may have just wasted your money.

Precautions

You may be familiar with the story of the woman who sued an online dating site because she was stabbed and nearly killed by a man who she met using their dating site. In case you're not familiar with the story, the man met the woman online and they went out on several dates. But things didn't work out; the woman didn't feel the spark was there. Three months later, the man waited in the woman's garage until she returned from work, then he stabbed her multiple times. After the knife broke, he repeatedly kicked her in the head and left her close to death.

The point of telling you that story is to make you listen — really listen—when I advise you to use common sense when dating.

It's pretty normal for people to have concerns about others they may meet when using online dating sites. Men and women generally have different concerns: women often joke about their fear of meeting a serial killer, and men more frequently want to avoid meeting "clingy" women, who can come off as aggressive, suffocating or stalking. Both men and women generally want to avoid meeting a person who is mentally unbalanced.

Be Realistic

Unfortunately, bad things happen, and they do not happen only online. Psychopaths exist; they always will, and they can be anywhere. Do you think the people you might meet at a bar would be any more psychologically stable than the people you might meet online? The answer is, they aren't (necessarily).

There are pros and cons to both meeting in a bar environment versus at an online dating site; but, at either location, people always have the opportunity to lie.

I've noticed in books, articles, interviews and seminars

that dating advisors often create rules intended to restrict daters from making common mistakes, such as exposing themselves to danger and vulnerabilities. While setting rules for yourself can restrict you from doing what feels natural, there must be guidelines to protect you from innocent mistakes that can result in regret or, even worse, danger.

Warnings for All Daters

- *Do not give out your physical address* to someone unless you've been out *at least* a few times. And when you do, make sure someone else knows about your meeting.

  If you give your home or work address to someone before meeting, you're asking for trouble. If you give someone your address too quickly, it sends the wrong message. Plus, it's always more intriguing when there's some degree of challenge and mystery. I'm not necessarily referring to sex, but the idea of setting the stage for intimacy, as in having complete privacy, is a risk.

  I certainly wouldn't frown on taking a risk, but you shouldn't take risks with someone you don't have a good feeling about—go out at least two or three times to get a feel for your chemistry together. Remember: If you invite someone over to your home, you will be stuck with that person—alone—until they leave.

- *Don't share private information*—such as your Social Security Number.

  You may think it would be common knowledge, but apparently it's not. Do know that identity theft is prevalent, and providing your Social Security Number to anyone other than a health professional, bank representative, accountant or credit card representative is *a really bad idea*.

- *Don't invite someone to your home* unless:

  You've been out a few times (you enjoy each other's company)

  You have really good chemistry

  You have a good feeling about them

- *Don't give someone access to your Facebook account* unless you feel comfortable that they will not violate your privacy.

- *Do not walk down a dark alley* alone with someone on a first date.

Your Profile

Think of your quest for companionship as a job search. Your dating-website *profile* can be thought of as your dating résumé. It therefore deserves a captivating description that accentuates your best features and presents you as aesthetically pleasing. If you create a great profile, it will greatly improve your odds of success. On the flip side, if you put little effort into creating your profile, your results will likely reflect that. It isn't logical to expect different results than the competition unless your profile differs from theirs, so don't simply read others' profiles and pattern yours after theirs. Be original.

Pictures

Think of online dating as window shopping. Daters will want to open the door and browse further only if you get their attention, and your pictures are crucial to getting a dater's attention. Note that I say "pictures," not "picture." The more pictures, the better; however, quality is always more important than quantity.

Be honest, but be smart. Your pictures are the first visual impression daters will have of you. You probably shouldn't use pictures more than two years old because your weight has likely fluctuated by more than a few noticeable pounds, your face has aged a bit, or you just simply look older. Get over it and get some fresh shots taken. When dating, you always want to put your best "face" forward, and the best way to do so is to be genuine from the start, beginning with your profile photos. It's understood you want to show pictures of your sexy body from college in your favorite bathing suit or the six pack that you used to have, but if you don't look like that anymore, don't be misleading. You can be successful if you focus on your current positive attributes.

Clothing matters. If possible, show examples of you dressed formally as well as casually—no mug shots. If you think it's cool to look "gangsta," it's not. Really, I assure you it's not. Regardless of what you think may be in style in your neck of the woods, wearing sagging pants, clothing that doesn't fit (too loose or too tight), or an outfit that is not flattering will more than likely be counterproductive and may result in few or no messages for you. On a related note, don't post a picture of yourself flexing or posing provocatively in a mirror—especially at a gym. It's a bad move, truthfully. If you feel insulted or embarrassed because I just called you out—don't; instead, just take my advice. It has worked for me, many of my friends and every one of my private clients thus far. There is no shame in seeking fashion consulting advice. Many people do it. The biggest mistake you can make is to send the wrong signal with a misleading image.

Guys, if your photo shows you as a player (someone in it only for the hookups) you may have some success in attracting a certain type of dater, but you may find it's an obstacle in establishing or maintaining a meaningful relationship. Either way, if you are reading this book, what you have been doing hasn't been working for you—that means it's time for a change. It doesn't mean you should go from one extreme to the next and start dressing ultra-conservatively, but if you want to attract someone who seeks more than a meaningless fling, you shouldn't give others the sense that you're a player.

Girls, the same goes for you. Looking sexy is great, but sending out the wrong signals will attract the wrong potential matches, for the wrong reasons, and will likely yield unwanted results. There is no need to use pictures that are overly conservative, but pictures that are overtly suggestive will likely send out the wrong signals. Blatantly short skirts or excessive cleavage is not an effective way to attract someone to your heart. Moderation is key.

Guys and girls: smile in at least some of your pictures. The positive energy of a smile is a great way to attract companionship. If you feel lonely, know that looking lonely or forlorn is not going to help you attract others.

Don't post pictures of yourself with an ex; it's not appropriate. If the best picture of you happens to be from a vacation with your ex, use common sense and crop it. The focus of your profile should be on you. Keep that in mind for all your pictures; don't confuse potential matches by using photos with groups of people. Anyone viewing your profile pictures should be able to identify you effortlessly.

Writing About Yourself

You need to be original when you describe yourself. Try not to seem like everyone else—don't be generic. If you are too proud to hire someone like me to help create your profile, you will need to research your online dating competition; I encourage you to review other daters' profiles. Read what they have written and note what you like, and don't like, in certain profiles. Yes, that means you should view your competitors' profiles. I suggest you log in as a "guest" user (if it's an option) to avoid giving your competitors the sense that you're interested in them but will allow you to browse anonymously.

I do not recommend limiting your "about me" section to cliché, beauty pageant quotes, such as "I like spending time with my friends and family" or "taking long walks on the beach." Guess what? Most people like spending time with their friends—it doesn't make you seem original. Believe me, no one is going to read your profile, come across "I like spending time with my friends" and think to themselves, *Oh, my god. Wow! We have so much in common.*

A successful profile needs to accomplish two things:

1. Attract people to view your profile (get them there)
2. Describe yourself captivatingly (keep them there)

Using a word-processing program, such as Word, you can create a new document then "copy" and "paste" each of the profile questionnaire fields into the document. This allows you to develop and polish your profile while you're offline, at your leisure. Once you're pleased with what you've created, you can copy the information into your online profile within the respective profile fields.

Picking Online Dating Website(s)

There is no need to limit yourself to one online dating website, but each one is different. First, be honest with yourself and decide what is important to you regarding your potential match. Religion, race, ethnicity, cultural background, language barriers or other important considerations can be deal breakers. If you are open only to dating someone who is Christian, then choosing JDate, which is intended for Jewish daters, isn't going to be an effective use of your time. To save both you and your potential matches from unneeded disappointment or frustration, I recommend you figure out your deal breakers before you connect with anyone. One place to start is the list of sites in Appendix C: *Online Dating Sites.*

Since each website is different, test out the ones that intrigue you. You can likely create a profile and select preferences to browse through each website's database of matches at no cost. As you familiarize yourself with a website's user functionality and tools, the time you spend will become increasingly more productive. You may eventually find focusing your energy and time on fewer, or even just one, site may improve your success rate. While dating is a numbers game, efficient website navigation and communication plays a crucial role.

Communicating

In your research, you may find that some online dating websites do not feature an instant messaging tool. In that case, there's probably an option to e-mail users, or, of course, you can check out different websites and find one that offers IM.

Before you start IM-ing users, if you're not already familiar with IM lingo, I highly recommend that you get familiar. You can start by reviewing Appendix A: *Abbreviations and Emoticons*, which presents a list of basic abbreviations, acronyms and emoticons. Instant message dialog can move really fast, and if you are constantly looking up acronyms or asking what terms mean, you may quickly lose an IM-er's interest and get frustrated.

Here are some examples of commonly used IM lingo:

- brb: be right back
- g/g or g2g or gg: gotta go/got to go

- np: no problem
- nm: not much
- btw: by the way

For further reading material on creating a great online dating profile, I recommend:

- *Love at First Click: The Ultimate Guide to Online Dating* by Laurie Davis
- *Modern Dating: A Field Guide* by Chiara Atik

An IM tool's functionality will likely vary from site to site. For example, some dating websites' IM tool may feature an audio/video (A/V) chat option, which, when activated, allows you and the other person to see and hear each other while you communicate. You need to know that if you choose to enable an A/V chat feature, you will no longer be IM-ing; instead, it would be considered a real-time web conference. If you find A/V intimidating, simply don't use it.

For anyone who thinks IM is intimidating, an A/V chat can be substantially more so; if you stutter, stammer, burp or fart, the other person will hear it, and if you twitch, squirm, roll your eyes or blush, they will see it. However, no one can force you to participate in an A/V chat. If you communicate with someone who requests you transition to an A/V chat scenario, and you are not comfortable with it, just respectfully decline. "I'd prefer to chat a bit more and get better acquainted before we jump to that," you might tell the other person. Remember, there's nothing wrong with saying, "No," especially when it's done politely.

The various website tools were developed to help online daters create *social context*, which is a socially comfortable environment. For example, many dating websites feature a tool that enables users to passively inform other users they are intrigued by the other's profile, which serves as a means to initiate communication by IM. While some people are comfortable beginning a conversation with a complete stranger, others see it as a great obstacle. Your comfort level will dictate your use of dating website tools.

When someone you're interested in logs on to the dating site while you are not around, there are usually only two means by which you can get their attention:

1. The chance they might stumble upon your profile while browsing for matches. Keep in mind that some people only log on to their accounts during off-peak hours (i.e. early morning or late night).

2. They are notified of your interest because you used a tool to express it.

I recommend you familiarize yourself with every tool and feature offered by the website(s) you choose to use. You may find some are beneficial. For website-specific IM tool instructions, consult customer service and support for the website(s) in question. If you cannot find tool-specific instructions at a particular website, there will likely be a customer-support phone number to call for further assistance. Do not be shy—support staff are there to help you succeed on their website. If there is customer support available to answer calls, you're not the only one dialing in . . . you're not alone.

Almost everyone texts, but there is a significant difference between a text conversation outside of a dating website and an ongoing IM conversation within one. I do not recommend approaching a text message conversation the same way you would approach IM. And, as I mention in the coming chapter, I do not recommend extensive follow-up text or phone conversations until rapport has been established via IM because they are very different communication vehicles. While a typical IM conversation takes place within an uninterrupted setting, a text message conversation typically consists of brief, intermittent communication exchanges throughout an extended time span.

Before You Send Your First IM

Before you begin to communicate with another online dater, you must understand the benefit of first developing your IM strategy. You must be enthusiastic *about* IM-ing to reveal genuine enthusiasm *when* IM-ing. Remember, enthusiasm is contagious. An IM conversation can be either an obstacle that hinders success or an extremely resourceful way to get a date. With harnessed skills, it's a nearly fail-proof way to create context for a genuine *social foundation*, best described as a comfortable communication environment.

Outside of IM, it's far more challenging to approach people. Men are often too afraid to approach women in person for various reasons: fear of rejection, fear of the girl's friends' rejection or fear of people witnessing your rejection. IM can eliminate almost all of your fears. But don't think of IM-ing as an easy way out or a way to take short cuts; just think of it as being resourceful.

Rather than simply memorizing and reproducing my responses in coming chapters, you should understand the theory behind them so you can learn to craft responses consistent with your personality. Then you can begin to direct the flow of an IM conversation. The ultimate benefit of developing an IM strategy is that your conversation will affect how you are perceived when you meet.

It's easy to reinforce your IM persona with consistent

behavior—as long as you are being yourself. Behind a computer screen you can visually disguise all potential unattractive insecurities, such as nervousness, initial fear of rejection, shaking, hesitations and awkwardness. Be original. Be funny. Be witty. Be smart. Be honest. Most importantly, always be confident. If you don't ask, you may likely never get the sale—in this case, the phone number, the mutual desire to communicate further and the in-person date.

This book is based on the knowledge I acquired over more than nine years of online dating experience, during which I analyzed my personal endeavors. I don't necessarily know more than everyone else, but I have taken the time to connect the dots of early communications that led to the exchanging of phone numbers and the mutual desire to meet or communicate further. In combining extensive experience with my professional sales background, I have formulated and tested theories in real-time IM conversations and e-mail communications.

This book's strategy development involves:

- Establishing an initial energy, getting someone's undivided attention
- Providing an explanation of my response to IMs
- Choosing a response choice and why
- Utilizing a topic transition
- Developing a mental connection
- Building enthusiastic energy
- Shifting conversational energy and balance
- Creating the base for initial trust
- Disagreeing without arguing

- Suggesting a phone call as a segue to getting the phone number and avoiding rejection

Individual elements of conversations include:

- What to talk about
- How to make jokes and what's acceptable
- How to emanate charisma and develop style
- What to avoid talking about
- How to answer awkward questions and avoid answers discretely
- How to improvise when things get awkward

This book will show various examples based on actual, real-time IM conversations that took place on dating websites. Naturally, all personal information has been removed to thoroughly conceal the women's identities. While my interactions in the book were with women, this book's theories, strategies, reasoning, rationales, and respective explanations and generalizations are applicable to most ethnic and religious backgrounds and sexual preferences.

Because my online dating experiences were with women, I will use "she" and "her" to describe them.

Chapter 1

Conversation with Cassandra:
Building a Social Foundation

As I have said before and will continue to tell you, the dating process is essentially an interview—because monogamy leaves room for only one person to be chosen. This first chapter serves as an example of a successful conversation with a girl I'll call Cassandra. My conversation with Cassandra incorporates a variety of diverse strategies, which will be analyzed in further depth in the chapters to come. The following IM exchange is an example of first contact with Cassandra after I reviewed her profile and decided she was the kind of person I'd like to get to know. As you will read, we eventually express a mutual desire to communicate further and meet, and she gives me her phone number.

Preparing for Communication

Before you contact someone whose profile has intrigued you, take the time to review the profile thoroughly. As I wrote in the introduction, you should literally study it. Why study a person's profile if you intend to communicate with them? For the same reason you study a company, person or position for which or with whom you will interview. Doing so enables you to ask intelligent and thought-provoking questions.

When communicating with someone, a great way to be captivating is to engage them in conversation. Theoretically, a person's favorite topic in a conversation is—them. A smart way to get someone's undivided attention is to make that person feel special. If you can make them feel special, they will likely be happy to give you attention.

One way to make a person feel special is to ask them about specific points in their profile. For example, if you learn something interesting about them, such as they speak multiple languages, have traveled the world, love pets, have gone skydiving or studied abroad, you should ask about it and use it to create *conversational context*, a recipe to foster thought-provoking dialog. If you see something funny or interesting in the pictures a person has posted, bring that up as well. I recommend using any information or pictures that you find funny or interesting in a person's profile to create conversational context.

The more you ask about someone and show interest in what they say, the more interesting you will seem. They should eventually try to learn about you, but if that doesn't happen, you might want to reconsider your interest in them. The more you know about one another, the more social context there should be.

IM-ing with Cassandra

IM-er: hey there

<<<<<<< Waiting to Connect >>>>>>>

Believe it or not, your introductory line is really important. Every subtlety makes a difference. The way you write your introduction sets the stage for the initial "vibe" between the two of you.

"Hello" can come off as silly because it's not a commonly used greeting unless you're on the phone and no one is answering on the other end. It's generally only used as, "Hello? Hello?" Further, hello is more of a formal greeting. Within a dating circumstance, people should act as casual and comfortable as possible to help set the tone.

"Hey" comes off as a basic, safe opener. That's because it's a very common, casual greeting in American English, and it seems soft and harmless. However, "hey!" and of course "Hey!" both come off as accentuated enthusiasm. In fact, the more capitalized letters you include, the bolder your IM becomes. But be careful with writing in ALL CAPS and using too many exclamation points. Doing so can often make your words seem overbearing, intense and akin to shouting.

Similar to "hey" but slightly less causal is "Hi." For example, in a business scenario, "Hi" would generally be a more common greeting than "Hey" because "Hey" is a seemingly more casual greeting than "Hi." When you add "!" or CAPS, increased enthusiasm and energy are associated.

If you consider yourself a high energy, enthusiastic

and socially confident person, I suggest saying "Hi there" or "Hey there." When adding "there," it creates a more flirtatious, confidently aggressive tone. By adding "there," it's almost as if you're saying, "You, look over here. I have something important to tell you." If you have enthusiastic energy, these are great openers.

Finally, "Hey you" is the most flirtatious and aggressive of all. Don't use this opener in a first conversation because the "you" insinuates a familiar tone.

IM-er: I'm Keith

It's essential to keep in mind if a person opens or acknowledges the IM you have sent, it's a spontaneous date. This gives you the ability to create the context of a first date before your first in-person date. If you make a good impression on your first IM date, the person will feel much more enthusiastic and comfortable on your first in-person date than they would otherwise. To achieve that goal, your conversation should reflect the flow of a face-to-face conversation; try to type as closely as possible to the speed at which you think. Remember too that some sites may require your potential matches to "accept" an IM (similar to how many cell phones require users to "answer" a call in order for the recipient to greet the caller) before the recipient can read and respond to the message.

<<<<<<< Waiting to Connect >>>>>>>

IM-er: I think you have an adorable smile

Be bold! If she connects with you, your opening is your opportunity not only to get her attention but to keep it. Make her smile, or laugh, as long as you are making her react. There needs to be an energy flow within a conversation. Intrigue her to respond. Engage her. You can compliment her or make a joke associated with her profile. *But do not lie to achieve that goal.* When I told Cassandra she had an adorable smile, I meant it; I'd visited her profile prior to sending the IM.

<<<<<<< Waiting to Connect >>>>>>>

<<<<<<< Connected >>>>>>>

Girl: hi Keith, i'm Cassandra
Girl: thanks :)
IM-er: You're welcome, Cassandra

It's always important to acknowledge a person by using their first name. Doing so will make them feel more comfortable, and it will help you become more familiar with their name, allowing you to associate the name with the right person. Be sure to spell it correctly.

IM-er: I rarely meet girls named Cassandra . . . I like that name

Now that you've been bold, be consistent. You must keep it up and keep her attention. Give genuine compliments, but when you do, be cognizant of your verbiage. For example, use "I rarely" instead of "I never"—it sounds more genuine. Follow through

on compliments: "and I like that name." Every obser-
vational statement that you make about her should
be directly or indirectly a compliment, even if it's a
backhanded compliment, also referred to as a "neg,"
which will be explained in greater detail later in the
book. Vary your grammar when expressing yourself
the same way you would if it were a spoken-word
conversation.

IM-er: :-)

It's important to express yourself with as much
variety as possible. Use emoticons (see a smile
emoticon, above), vocabulary, word play, grammar,
etc., but never too much of anything. Go the extra
mile. Get completely involved in the conversation.
Common emoticons can be found in Appendix A:
Abbreviations and Emoticons.

Don't just write to her, *speak* to her as if you were
talking. Type it exactly as you would say it, but use
proper grammar and punctuation. By proper I don't
mean formal. For example, you don't necessarily
have to begin your sentences with capital letters. Remember, this is conversational text. However, it works
to your advantage to show that you have a command
of your language. If you spell correctly and use apos-
trophes and commas appropriately, you seem more
intelligent.

IM-er: yes, these are legitimate compliments

If you're giving many compliments, you can call
yourself out by commenting on the things you're
saying: "these are legitimate compliments." Doing
so may help you avoid seeming phoney.

Girl: haha
Girl: well, I don't know many Keiths either
IM-er: well, I'm going to hope that's a good thing
IM-er: hopefully I can make it a good thing
IM-er: that will be my goal

React to reciprocated compliments or other positive feedback. You can subtly reinforce commentary by showing enthusiasm or by simply reacting to it. When you make cute, witty commentary, give her a chance to react to it. A witty back and forth is a far greater achievement than a one-sided, witty comeback. In a perfect situation, everything would be 50/50.

Girl: sounds like a good game plan
IM-er: haha
IM-er: although, of all your pics . . . the most adorable is the expression on your face in the 3rd
Girl: haha, my friend just grabbed my ass and picked me up, it was great timing on the pic
IM-er: haha
IM-er: so, that's how you react when your ass is grabbed?

She reacts, so YOU react.

Stay involved. Don't start with boring questions such as, "What do you do?" or, "Where'd you go to school?" It's counterproductive. Your goal is to make her interested in you. She should want to ask you questions, so you have to make it fun. Point out something that strikes your interest. Anything that is particularly cute or different.

If she gives you a chance to be cute or a wiseass or clever, take it! You are being tested. She will not be interested unless you are interesting.

Be funny. If she brings up her "ass," make a comment referring to it too. It's an open invitation to be respectfully flirtatious.

Remember to always express yourself as if this were a face-to-face conversation; essentially, it is. You're both looking at a screen and both typing— you're looking at one another via computer screens, just not necessarily with real-time video. It's very important to express everything you write at a speed relative to the speed you would speak. If you need to bone up on your keyboarding skills, do so *before* you start your online dating quest.

IM-er: lol
Girl: yes-that exact face every time
IM-er: noted-lol

If she's a wiseass to you, be a wiseass back. A man needs to maintain an edge. And, if she's sarcastic, then you have to make your retort quickly. Wit is always a turn-on and is always impressive.

Make a quick recovery. If you can't think of anything very interesting, you can jump back to the basics, such as asking where she's from, what she does, etc. But when you discuss generic subjects, make sure your word choice is as original as possible; it makes you seem more genuine. You need to keep her asking questions too. It's easy to keep the conversation going when you're asking the questions because she will likely follow up her answers by re-directing the questions back at you.

IM-er: so, where are you originally from?
Girl: well, i've been living in Brooklyn over 8 years now

Girl: so i'm going to say Brooklyn, haha
Girl: I grew up in Memphis
Girl: where are you from?
IM-er: :-) I grew up in Westchester County

Now that she has come back with the same question, you need to keep her interested and keep her responding. Find something to spark a discussion. You should try to find things in common; it makes for an interesting conversation and is an easy way to connect with someone.

IM-er: I asked because I see that you speak French
IM-er: a beautiful language
Girl: ohh . . . !

Ellipses, and especially exclamation points, are very expressive forms of punctuation. Ellipses (...) are very different from exclamation points (!). Within the context of IM, ellipses can be used to indicate an extended pause or an ongoing thought. Either way, use of punctuation demonstrates a person's effort to apply symbols to their conscious expressions. Exclamation points indicate energy and enthusiasm, and it can mean a raised voice. Use of these punctuation marks is an ideal indication that the person with whom you're speaking is actively engaged in the conversation.

Note how, when I pointed out I realize she speaks French, she responded with an enthusiastic "oh . . . !" This is a perfect example of why it's so helpful to review and study a person's profile and to provide interesting details in your profile. Any interesting and unique details someone may read about you in your profile (languages, travel experiences, hobbies,

skills) will improve your odds of distinguishing yourself from your competition.

Girl: yes, well my dad moved to Memphis from Quebec,
          went to hs in Quebec
Girl: so i picked up a bit of french, unfortunately don't get to
          use it too much anymore
IM-er: well, maybe you can use it with me
IM-er: I'm starting to learn it

It's good to be corny at times. But ultimately your
goal, from the very first conversation, is to establish
her interest in your personality based on an accu-
rate portrayal of yourself. If she is intrigued by your
IM personality but not by your real personality, it's
pointless. However, if she's intrigued by your IM personality, which is a reflection of the way you act in
person, it will likely affect the way she perceives you
in person.

Throw in random, cute commentary: occasional
little corny things, even if she doesn't respond. If after a few times, she don't acknowledge it as cute,
or doesn't respond at all, then don't continue to do
it. In this case, you would have to gage her reaction
in person. It's too risky to overdo things via IM because if you don't keep the person's interest, they
may choose to end the conversation. It's far easier
and less awkward to end an IM conversation than it
is to end an in-person date. It's always smart to follow
up a cute or corny comment with a transitional comment that brings you back to the main conversation.

Girl: do you speak any other languages?
Girl: tu parles francais?
IM-er: I speak Spanish and Italian

Girl: tres bien
Girl: prego
Girl: i looove italy

When duplicated letters are used to emphasize the way a word is expressed, such as "looove" above, pay attention. Even though she isn't commenting on you, she is still making the effort to be expressive with you, so she is giving you clues and hints. Pay attention and react. But never bring up something that you can't back up. If you say you can do something, be prepared to prove it.

IM-er: je aprende Francais petit a petit
IM-er: oui, tres bien
IM-er: trop bien
IM-er: :-)
Girl: ha, i always wished i learned spanish though
Girl: it's a much more useful language
IM-er: Yea . . . but I think French is super sexy
IM-er: it just is
IM-er: ya know?

Don't go out of your way to be agreeable if you don't agree. Although it is more challenging to do so, if you disagree, it's a sign of confidence. You need to stand by your opinions.

It's always more impressive to get her to agree with you. In any circumstance, if you share an opinion but then immediately agree with someone else's opinion instead, you seem like a follower, which is never attractive. A mature woman generally wants a man with a mind of his own.

Girl: i hear ya, but italian also

> When speaking to someone with a personality, but who also has opinions, you may notice she wants to be right. Don't necessarily argue, but stay true to your opinions, no matter how trivial they may be. It's not necessarily the importance of the topic that's relevant, it's maintaining a confident aura.

IM-er: true
IM-er: very true
IM-er: but, I'm very comfortable with Italian
IM-er: lol

> It's certainly not bad to agree, but respectfully stick to your opinion. Try to change your tactics from time to time. Use different words and expressions to present genuine opinions, yet don't be obnoxious. If you seem extreme, she may think you're a weirdo. Don't be too aggressive with your wording unless you need to be. Also, try to follow up any differences of opinion with a funny comment, which often takes away any awkwardness in the conversation.

IM-er: so, now I'm spoiled by it
IM-er: :-p
IM-er: so, I see we're both Libras

> Don't belabor the point. Find an opportunity to change the subject. Always look for things to say that make you seem attentive. Remember, everyone generally thinks about himself or herself. So give her a chance to speak about herself as often as possible. Be a good listener. "So, now I'm spoiled . . ." is a

humorous comment that gives her something else to comment on.

IM-er: when's your bday?
IM-er: (not that I know much about this astrology stuff)

Most likely, she's first going to react to the joke ("So, now I'm spoiled . . ."). Then, she'll probably jump on the subject change.

Girl: ha, italian is something good to be spoiled by, i'd like to be spoiled by italian
Girl: i guess it means we're both balanced? or so they say
Girl: oct 11
Girl: you?
IM-er: oct. 3rd
IM-er: that means I get gifts first :-p

If it feels natural, be funny and cute. Regardless, always try to be quickly perceptive. It's good to be playful with a quick-witted comment like "that means I get gifts first :p." If possible, it's a very powerful technique to establish playful banter via an IM conversation because it sets the stage for a playful and comfortable rapport when you meet in person.

IM-er: lol
Girl: yes, but my birthday is always during baseball playoffs
Girl: and being a yankees fan . . . .
IM-er: haha, good
IM-er: me too
Girl: it's like extra presents every year
IM-er: haha
IM-er: I can tell that you're a fun girl already

Girl: that's what they all say ;)

Throw in random compliments, especially if they come out naturally. If the girl is sparking your interest, let her know. It will make her feel good. If she's fun, tell her she's fun. No need to tell someone 1,000 times that she's beautiful or has gorgeous eyes, but if she seems like a fun, charismatic person, definitely let her know.

IM-er: so . . . can I ask you a few corny questions?

If you're going to be corny, and you know you're going to seem corny, it can be an effective strategy to call yourself out on it. Being aware of your corniness makes it seem inherently less corny. This is self deprecation and is a great way to establish your vulnerability, which can be described as exposure of personal emotions and feelings to others. But remember, once you decide to go the corny route, you must play it out. Once you talk about doing something, be prepared to do it.

Girl: haha "what do you like to do for fun?"
IM-er: no no . . .
IM-er: that's awful
Girl: i hate those questions
IM-er: well . . . give me . . . 2

Rather than feeding off of her negativity, I stayed strong and kindly demanded ". . . give me . . . 2." This shows that I have no shame in being a bit corny, and she will like my confidence.

Girl: haha, ok, well you just passed the cool test

Girl: go for it
IM-er: ok . . . before anything, I must ask . . . do you mind
         dating a guy who doesn't keep kosher?

You will note, based on my above reference to "kosher," that I was actively communicating with a Jewish girl. You can filter your online dating matches based on such preferences.

When you ask a corny question, make sure it has a reason behind it. Make sure your corniness isn't in the question itself but in the way you ask it. It's just a way to establish a cute-guy vibe. In my experience, girls do generally seem to like guys who come off as assholes, but they don't want to get seriously involved with them; they want to end up with a good guy who can keep them interested.

Girl: is there bacon involved?
Girl: ;)
Girl: i dont mind at all—my parents do keep kosher, but i
         haven't really kept it since i started college
IM-er: perfect
IM-er: a winner . . .
IM-er: you come from the traditional background, with those
         good-girl values
IM-er: but, don't mind
IM-er: lol

If you get the answer that you want, show enthusiasm. Your enthusiasm will feed her enthusiasm. If you show excitement, she's more likely to be excited.

Girl: pretty much sums it up
IM-er: by the way . . . of course bacon . . . all guys love 'the pork'

IM-er: :-p

Take occasional risks. To stand out from the crowd, you have to be willing to take risks. Be willing to make occasional witty, risky jokes. If and when you do, be prepared to wait 20–25 seconds before getting a response. If you don't get a response, you may have to try to soften the blow.

Girl: haha
Girl: how can you not?
IM-er: dunno
IM-er: dunno . . .
IM-er: lol
IM-er: ok . . .
IM-er: 2 true corny questions
IM-er: and that's it

When being self-deprecating, remember, the best offense is a good defense. So, defend what you say. It is a display of confidence and yet subtly avoids any likely association with seeming cocky or arrogant. It's important that you establish your vulnerability: if the girl reveals it *for* you, you lose control of the balance.

Girl: so that was one, what is number 2?
IM-er: that wasn't corny . . . that was legit

Again, remember to always be ready to defend your claims, comments and questions. Be just as willing to call yourself out on stupidity and corniness as you are prepared to defend what you say.

IM-er: lol
Girl: well, food is a very important topic, so I'll give you that
        one

    Don't ever expect the girl to agree with you without hesitation; she'll likely preface her agreement with "Well." But either way, her agreement is a very good accomplishment. Balance is now established.

IM-er: see, we agree

    Don't take a cocky tone. Just accept your victory graciously.

IM-er: d'ccord
IM-er: lol
IM-er: ok
IM-er: 1.) . . .
Girl: prego
IM-er: hey, that was frecnh
IM-er: *French
IM-er: guess I=not
IM-er: lol
IM-er: *guess not

    You will note that these are mistakes. Yes, this is a published book with blatant mistakes—because people make mistakes. It's probably going to happen to you eventually, especially within the context of an IM conversation. It's not the end of the world if you make typos here and there or even misspell a word. When you catch your mistakes, you can always correct yourself by sending a follow-up IM with your correction.

    If you wish to emphasize that you are making a

correction so the person doesn't confuse your correction with repeating yourself, you can preface your correction with an asterisk (*).

IM-er: okok . . . 1.)
IM-er: what are your defining personality characteristics . . .
        i.e. sweet, caring, affectionate, compromising . . . etc?

Like all first dates, it is always, in some way, an interview. You should ask at least a few real questions, even if they seem generic and corny. Do so only after establishing rapport, because it shows genuine interest.

Girl: hmm--i'd say sweet/playful. i don't have much patience
        for bs
Girl: but i will do pretty much anything for my friends and
        family
Girl: what would you say yours are my fellow libra
IM-er: wait, wait . . .
IM-er: lol
IM-er: you didn't address those specifically :-p

Show confidence. If you want to say something, find a way to say it. If you want to ask something, find a way of asking it. If you ask a question, but she doesn't completely answer it, call her out on it. This shows sternness and confidence, which are attractive characteristics.

IM-er: so . . . sweet, yes . . . caring . . . yes, affectionate?
        Compromising?
Girl: affectionate yes, compromising—hmm, it depends on
        the situation
Girl: i'm not gonna pretend that i'll go 50/50 on every

disagreement to make it fair
IM-er: I only ask . . . because compromising is one of the most
important characteristics to make a relationship work
IM-er: and . . . you know it's true

When asking a corny question, it is crucial to have an explanation for why you asked so you can define why it's important to you. When you make the effort to be genuine and defend your statements, it will be noticed and generally respected.

Girl: that explains a lot ;)
IM-er: well . . . ya gotta agree on that . . . no?
IM-er: lol

If discussing your views regarding the importance of compromising, it's essential to point out that you agree—if you agree—and, in this case, express enthusiasm.

Girl: it's important, and i usually advocate the middle of the
road in general
IM-er: ok, we have a winner
IM-er: ;-)
IM-er: your turn
Girl: are you giving up your second question?
IM-er: no
IM-er: just taking turns
IM-er: lol

In this situation, Cassandra is taking the initiative. She is showing involvement in the conversation by calling me out for not asking a second question. This is what you hope for; it is an indication of active engagement and interest.

Be quick and witty if she challenges you or calls you out on something. As always, be bold when you can. If she challenges you or calls you out on anything, be prepared to make a quick-witted joke.

Girl: is this a demonstration of "compromising"?
Girl: haha

If she's going to challenge you or call you out in one circumstance, she will likely do it in another, which should be an incentive to prepare yourself.

IM-er: haha
IM-er: it's certainly a display of some of my characteristics
Girl: ha, very nice
Girl: hmmm
IM-er: gotta be some things you want to know . . .
IM-er: lol
IM-er: I could think of a lot of questions to ask you
IM-er: but, maybe I don't want to make it that easy for you
IM-er: lol

Calling the girl out on things she says can be an effective way to show confidence, but never go overboard. If she pulls back, you should pull back a bit as well. Balance is important to maintain.

Try to switch the focus of the topic back to her as often as possible. Try to slip a witty joke into your comment, to be subtle: "but, maybe I don't want to make it that easy for you." Just be creative in expressing thoughts as often as possible. Every positive thing you do that makes you stand out from your competition will give you an edge.

Girl: ha, ok, well, keep asking, and i'll figure something out eventually

IM-er: fine . . . corny 2.)

IM-er: lol

IM-er: what are you looking for in a guy . . . personality-wise (cause I assume you saw my pics)

IM-er: ?

Girl: ha, i'd say someone that can keep up with me, sense of humor, intelligence but also a nice guy

Girl: i'm over the asshole phase ;)

Girl: what are you looking for in a girl?

You want her to ask you, "What are you looking for in a girl?" This is your chance to make her qualify herself for you. Be as specific as possible and be prepared to mention corny things, such as "cuddling."

IM-er: sweet, caring, affectionate, compromising, likes to get and give massages, would do anything with me . . . workout, go to the driving range, veg-out, lots of cuddling and enjoys good food with me

IM-er: obviously . . . cultured, intelligent and smart

Girl: ha, you have quite a well thought out answer, impressive

IM-er: I like silly too

IM-er: yes . . . I know

Girl: ha, how do you feel abt girls that are smarter than the guys they date?

IM-er: haha

For the most part, your responses should be as quick as possible. Take any opportunity to be a wiseass, because that is what allows you to go from just a nice guy to a nice guy with an edge.

IM-er: hmmm . . . as long as they aren't obnoxious
IM-er: lol
Girl: ha, so correcting spelling and grammar is a turn-off?
Girl: Haha
IM-er: lol
IM-er: depends . . .
Girl: :)
Girl: well, i actually need to head back to bed soon (i'm
         home sick, which is just awful in 100 degree weather),
IM-er: awww

Be sweet and be cute, but only if it's natural for you. Don't ever try to imitate me, because your best chance to succeed is to be yourself. If you find not everyone likes you—it's not a problem. And, for anyone who expects everyone will like you, let me save you the suspense: That's most likely not going to happen. But don't worry, you don't need everyone to like you. Ideally, you want the people you like to like you in return. So just concentrate on using my advice and suggestions to develop your own genuine IM style. As long as you're confident in yourself, you may find people who like you for being yourself.

IM-er: does that mean we have to stop talking :-(?
Girl: for right now, i have a sinus headache
IM-er: aww, I'm so sorry

At the end of a conversation, you must be prepared to make your move. Take the risk because you may never have another chance to "ask for the sale," and if you don't ask, it may be interpreted as lacking assertiveness, confidence and interest.

IM-er: well, I'm going to just be direct . . .

```
Girl:    thank you
IM-er:   when you are feeling better, I really want to meet you
IM-er:   I think you're awesome
Girl:    i'd like to meet you as well
Girl:    i have another 5 days on antibiotics
Girl:    so how abt next week sometime?
IM-er:   ok . . . I'd love to exchange numbers--and yes
IM-er:   next week will be perfect
Girl:    sure--my cell is ###-###-####
```

If you get the number, you're good to go as far as this conversation is concerned. When talking on the phone, be very careful, because too much communication before meeting can be a recipe for disaster. Excitement is great, and you want to be excited by this person, but too much of anything can be problematic. While there can always be exceptions, the three most likely outcomes of extensive pre-dating communications are:

1. *Best case* (not very common). You send each other frequent texts and/or talk on the phone often and for extended periods of time. Everything goes great. When you meet, there is a fantastic connection. You continue to date and communicate.

2. *Likely case.* You send each other frequent texts and/or talk on the phone often and for extended periods of time. Everything goes great. When you meet, one or both of you is disappointed by the other's appearance or feel that the person's online personality was not genuine. You do not continue dating.

3. *Worst case* (and most likely). You send each

other frequent texts and/or talk on the phone for extended periods of time. There no longer seems to be a connection; one or both of you is overly excited or nervous, which leads to acting out of character. You likely choose not to meet.

My advice is a gradual progression of communication. Begin with IM. Follow up the IM conversation with text messaging to transition to a phone call. Finally, meet in person.

While it is not necessarily common practice to save your IM conversations, I habitually did because I found it to be a fail-proof solution to remember the details from my conversations. Remembering details can be very helpful in creating social context, which is an important element of comfortable conversation.

IM-er: and btw . . . I see you're an engineer . . . I love an intellectual challenge . . . so yes, if you happen to be "smarter" I'll deal with it
Girl: done!
Girl: haha, i look forward to it
IM-er: :-)
IM-er: so do I
Girl: ok, i'm back to sleep
Girl: ttys
IM-er: feel better Cassandra . . . and we'll have some fun talking on the phone . . .
Girl: sounds good
IM-er: k, ttys sweet dreams
Girl: :)

<<<<<<< IM Conversation Ended >>>>>>>

The conversation with Cassandra is a great example of creating social foundation. Most girls are not going to go out of their way to be argumentative or mean—or overly nice. You can generally expect most women you speak to online to be somewhere right in the middle. Cassandra was very personable, which is why dissecting this conversation demonstrated how to create a successful social foundation. Not all people have bubbly, fun personalities, but by adapting your personality to a conversation, you can enable more compatibility.

Things did not work out with Cassandra because I felt compelled to overly communicate via text, which is a good example of how too much communication can be disastrous. Being excited and showing enthusiasm is ideal, but too much of anything is problematic. If you speak too much before you meet, it takes away the mystery. The goal of IM is to create context, which helps to warm up a cold scenario—just don't overheat it.

Do not get discouraged if things don't work out, because if you learn from your mistakes, things will only get better and easier with time.

Chapter 2

Conversation with Vanessa:
Shifting Balance

This chapter provides an example of Cassandra's opposite: Vanessa, a true challenge. A challenge can be very intriguing; in fact, I have always preferred a challenge. My advice to you is to avoid eliminating potential matches based on preconceived notions. Unless you are sure that someone isn't your type, at least keep an open mind. Don't avoid a challenge, because it could be exactly what you want. Within an IM conversation, a challenge means plenty of back-and-forth, quick-witted banter. It is difficult to know before contacting someone if they are going to challenge you; but, either way, you need to know that challenging them in return will be the only way to keep their interest.

The following will present actual shifts in balance and teach you how to reestablish and maintain balance within a dynamic environment. You will note that this chapter's IM strategy is different than what was presented in Chapter 1. Remember:

Every social exchange is different, and you must therefore appropriately approach every individual interaction.

IM-ing with Vanessa

IM-er: hey there

<<<<<<< Waiting to Connect >>>>>>>

IM-er: I think you're a classic beauty

This is a strong, affirmative introduction—as long as it's true.

<<<<<<< Connected >>>>>>>

Girl: y thank u

Her laziness (using "y" for "why" and "u" for "you") gives you an opportunity to seem sophisticated, but only if you choose to ignore her style. Despite her lazy typing, you should always put your best foot forward and use proper grammar. You will subtly seem more confident and intelligent, depending on your use of expressions, vocabulary and wit.

Further, writing "Y thank u" . . . or "why thank you" are both significantly more enthusiastic than "thank you" by itself. When a girl prefaces her response with "why" or "y" (which is generally associated with a question), she's almost giving you a heads-up, saying "ummm, just letting you know, I have a BIG personality, and I like to be EXTRA expressive."

Also, when a girl uses single letters in place of a word, such as Y, U or R, she's being lazy, which shows she isn't concerned with impressing you. Ignore her laziness. It will later serve you. I already know Vanessa is going to be a challenge, just based on her lazy typing.

Don't make the mistake of thinking she is uneducated just because she opts to be lazy with her typing. Be aware that her lazy typing indicates she isn't trying to impress you with the way she writes. She may likely not feel a pressing need to exchange contact information and, therefore, not make it easy to succeed. It can be a person's way of saying, "I don't really care," not necessarily because the person isn't interested in you, but because it may be a reflection of their easygoing nature. Ultimately, the best solution is to always try to intrigue your potential match, unless you decide you are disinterested and want to keep your distance.

Girl: dont worry i didnt add 30-40 lbs since the last pic hahaha

It's helpful to write something unique in your profile, such as making jokes or statements that may lead to someone's reaction. In my profile, I commented on how women don't always accurately represent themselves. Neither do men, by the way; many of us are guilty of dishonestly representing ourselves in one respect or another: height, weight, body type, accuracy of pictures and more. You may find people are often a lot heavier in person than their pictures lead you to believe. Including this type of commentary in your profile will help elicit conversation, because if she is chatting with you, she will likely read your profile.

IM-er: hahaha
Girl: maybe 10
IM-er: well, I'm amazed that you read my profile . . . .

> Often, the girl will make jokes that sometimes hint at her insecurities. It's generally not a good idea to react to a girl's insecurities via IM because the meanings of words can easily be lost in translation. Rather than react to a comment, it's good just to react to the situation. Instead of reacting to the "maybe 10," I instead reacted to the fact that she took the time to read my profile.

IM-er: I'm told it's a task lol

> It's important to set the tone to create a real dating atmosphere before you meet. Doing so helps develop a genuine social environment. For example, let her know that you're up to joking around. Build it up by letting the banter escalate. It doesn't hurt to make fun of yourself or call yourself out on little things, but in doing so, you need to be prepared to call out your potential match in a playful manner as well.
>
> For example, I called it "a task" to read my profile. I said that because I took the time to write a very detailed profile, and I knew anyone who read the majority of it would have likely spent at least five minutes doing so. While that may not sound like much time to spend reading someone's profile, you need to keep in mind that many profiles are often very brief—some nearly non-existent. Point is, since there are so many profiles to view, if a person spends the time to read yours, take it as a compliment. More importantly, give the person something to remember.

Girl: ill be honest, i check profiles for height lol

> This is a short girl—under five feet tall. So if she makes a comment about how dating a tall man is important to her, call her out on it. If a girl is going to challenge you, then she needs to know that you will challenge her in return; otherwise, she will become bored. You need to have an opinion, and it doesn't hurt to disagree—again, as long as you aren't obnoxious. It may give you the opportunity to break down her toughness if you can make her seem like she is being shallow. It's good to trigger the defenses of a challenger like Vanessa.

IM-er: haha
IM-er: so
IM-er: what's your preference?

> Notice how I wrote "so" Then, I wrote: "what's your preference?" I could have also written "so . . . what's your preference?" Either way would have set the same tone, prefacing the question with "so . . ." which is a good way to say, "really . . . ? That's interesting . . . I wouldn't expect that."

Girl: ur height or taller lol
IM-er: really?
IM-er: taller?
IM-er: lol

> It's not good to be obnoxious, but you should express your opinion. In a sense, she's already making it difficult for me by saying, ". . . or taller." She's under five feet tall so it's a bit shallow. Rather than get frustrated or discouraged, use it as an opportunity to

give her a taste of her own medicine.

Girl: yea lol used to tall guys for some reason last guy i
        dated was about 6 feet 2

"Used to" is her way of saying, "That's what I want, and that's what I'm going to get," so if you're going to react, be smooth about it. Keep the focus on her. When someone says something like that, it's important that your response elicits a response, or else you will likely find the conversation going stale.

IM-er: well, I imagine that a girl as beautiful as you is used to
        getting what she wants
IM-er: ;)

Now she's likely going to respond because I used her words, "used to," against her. In a sense, I put words into her mouth; but, that's not exactly what she said, so it will likely cause her to respond. I used the wink emoticon to let her know my comment was lighthearted in nature.

Girl: lol so not true!!!!
Girl: but thanks for the compliment ;)

Now that she has responded with enthusiasm (!!!!), there is a sense of balance between us. Once there is balance, you must keep it by maintaining your involvement in the conversation. There is no need to be overly enthusiastic, but it's best to reciprocate enthusiasm in your own way. If she uses very little grammar or punctuation, you can use less common vocabulary words.

IM-er: I'm flabbergasted
IM-er: oh, you're welcome . . . plenty more where that came from

"Plenty more where that came from" is a great way to express personality and edge through IM. It implies, "I can handle you." Since your matches can't hear your excitement, enthusiasm or sarcasm via your words alone, let them understand your enthusiasm using grammar, punctuation and, of course, expressions or wordplay.

Girl: lol
IM-er: so, I might as well go down the checklist here . . . :p
IM-er: does my not keeping kosher pose an issue?

If you're about to begin asking any boring or generic questions (as I suggested and explained earlier), call yourself out on it. It's a good defense because rather than giving them the chance to make fun of you, you're taking the initiative by doing it yourself. Beat them to the punch. You can refer to it as your "checklist" or filling out your "questionnaire." You can refer to it as anything that will give the sense that you know it's generic, which substantially softens the blow.

Girl: ure not jewish?

I will never know if she was seriously asking me this question (as if every Jew keeps kosher these days . . .), but a negative or hostile reaction from me would lead nowhere good. So, bite your tongue and respond calmly and directly to maintain balance.

IM-er: I'm Jewish
IM-er: just don't keep kosher
Girl: o thats fine
Girl: lol

Right back on track. She accepts my explanation, and there was only a momentary misunderstanding. However, if I had become angry and assumed she thought I was disgraceful and sacrilegious, the conversation would have become stale and she would have likely put an end to any opportunity I had.

Girl: neither do i
Girl: i just dont eat pork
IM-er: and if I do?

Remind her of whatever point you want to make. Never avoid making a point, just don't rub it in her face. This is a subtle reassurance of confidence. It's a way of saying, "This is what I'm going to do. How do you feel about that?"

Girl: whatever makes u happy

Her response can be interpreted one of three ways: 1) she is being a big wiseass, or 2) she is being serious, or 3) she is being serious while also being a wiseass. Either way, as long as there's no disagreement, move on with the conversation.

IM-er: well, I'm a carnivore . . . for sure
IM-er: and I'm a guy . . . so, I like the pork
IM-er: lol
IM-er: so, you seem like an anomaly . . .
IM-er: generally girls who I find to be as striking as you don't

come off as genuinely sweet girls . . . .
IM-er: but, you do

I certainly didn't think Vanessa was being sweet, although I thought she had an undeniably cute IM personality. Yes, you will note that I recycle my jokes, because if something works and is being done in a genuine way, why not go with it? Should you? Absolutely, as long as it's genuine. The reason I referred to her as "sweet" was to soften her up. She has a big guard up, and she's trying to make it difficult for me to succeed. So, if I can ignore her wiseass commentary and pretend I don't notice it, her guard will begin to lower a bit. And by using an adjective such as "sweet," it only encourages sweet behavior from her. In a way, I'm testing her to see if she's actually sweet.

Girl: its im, how can u tell?

This is a great question, and it calls you out. It allows you to seem perceptive. This is a challenge and an opportunity for you to try to give a genuine compliment. As discussed earlier, most people don't take IM seriously because they don't realize how powerful a tool it can be.

IM-er: your pics
IM-er: your smile
IM-er: only a sweet girl smiles the way you do
Girl: or a devil one

Vanessa is certainly a rare breed, so rather than taking the blatant compliment, she makes a wise crack ("or a devil one"). Be prepared to give a quick response in return. Remember, when dealing with a jokester, you have to be spontaneous. If she makes a wiseass comment, be prepared to comment back as quickly, if not quicker, than she does. That is what allows you to maintain the balance.

IM-er: they can coexist
Girl: be careful what u say ;)

It seems at this point in the conversation that Vanessa will not ease up. No matter how clever, quick or nice the things I say are, she has not softened up. But at least she's playful. Now she says, "be careful what u say." She's testing me. You cannot blow off a test. If she's going to be playful, then it's crucial to stand your ground.

IM-er: lol
Girl: hahahah
IM-er: I'm always careful with my words
IM-er: I never mince . . .
IM-er: yet, my assumptions and presumptions have a method to their madness
IM-er: I bet you can be feisty . . .
IM-er: but, willing to bet you tear during chick flicks
Girl: drama queen def, feisty eh not so much . . . .what chick doesnt cry during chick flicks?
Girl: i cry at everything lol im an emotional wreck

If she decides to test you, test her right back. Try to be intuitive. When I say, "I bet you can be feisty . . . but, willing to bet that you tear during chick flicks," that is where I begin what I refer to as *quid pro quo*. For those of you that aren't familiar with the expression, in Latin it means "this for that." And that's really what it is, but within the context of a conversation. The premise is to make an observation, judgment or assumption based on the social context that's been established. Quid pro quo: You make an observation, judgment or assumption, and, in return, you get positive reinforcement or learn useful information. The purpose is:

- If you're right, your match will likely tell you you're right, and you will demonstrate perceptiveness and conversational engagement, which means you will likely impress your match and create more social context.

- If you're wrong, your match will likely tell you you're wrong, but in doing so, you will have learned new information about your match, which helps create more social context.

Creating social context helps make the social interaction more comfortable, which in turn helps lower your match's guard.

She tested me, so I tested her back, and now she's dropping her guard a bit by revealing some level of vulnerability. That was the first really self-conscious comment Vanessa made: "im an emotional wreck." Even though she prefaced it with "lol," it was, by all means, serious.

IM-er: non-sweet ones
IM-er: only the ones with sweetness somewhere inside can be emotional
IM-er: unless you can think of a contradictory example
IM-er: . . .
IM-er: :p

If you found that quid pro quo helped lower her

guard, you could push it a bit further with another test or similar comment, which can help to lower her guard, little by little. Once you've stood your ground and established mutual agreement, you will have reached a balance.

The most powerful part of the second test was when I said, "unless you can think of a contradictory example." Notice that I was asking without the use of a question mark, which enabled me to pose a question in the form of a statement. That was a blatant challenge. By throwing that last part in there, it was like saying, "so, unless you can prove me wrong, please stop challenging me." While making smart aleck remarks can be an effective way to seem playful, there is a fine line between being playful and being obnoxious.

Girl: cant beat that!

Now that you've genuinely established conversational balance, there's no need to take advantage of it. But it can't hurt to check in on how you're doing.

IM-er: haha
IM-er: so, I'm not doing so badly here . . . am I?
Girl: so far, no ;)
IM-er: I get the sense that you make a guy work hard for your affection . . . but, when earned . . . you're a giver

You may be familiar with the term "neg," which is best described as a backhanded compliment. By its nature, a neg is half-compliment, half-insult. It is intended to trigger the recipient's ea- ger defense mechanism, compelling them to self-justify and/or self-qualify. A neg's delivery is the key to its effectiveness. An example of a neg within the context of IM is when I wrote, "I get the sense that you make a guy work hard for your affection . . . but, when earned . . . you're a giver."

Some may not consider that statement a neg in the traditional sense because the "backhanded" aspect is very subtle. While saying, "I get the sense that you make a guy work hard for your affection," is not a blatant insult, it is certainly a judgment and was not intended as a compliment. However, following up with "but, when earned . . . you're a giver," is complimentary. Again, the intention of the neg is to trigger a self-justifying and/or self-qualifying response.

As you will see, Vanessa responded with "no lol . . . im easy . . . hahahahah."

A neg can be a great way to shift conversational energy once balance has been established. Prior to meeting in person, I strongly advise against negging someone before social balance is established because the neg's delivery may be misinterpreted as an unwarranted insult. With that said, when negging someone via online dating, I would only recommend subtle negs, such as my example above.

Trying to go quid pro quo with a girl like Vanessa is a major challenge. She's not going to just hand out the answers you want. You will have to play a little hardball and some softball. You will have to hold your tongue at moments and be assertive at others.

Vanessa's example of quid pro quo is an attempt at being sweet and perceptive. Be cognizant of all her responses. You may very likely have to use her words to prove your points and to help yourself re-establish balance. It's important that you understand where the *conversational balance* lies. Conversational balance is a state of rapport in which the mutual

recognition of interest is established through reciprocal, active engagement. In an IM conversation, balance is constantly shifting. Every time you make a
comment you both don't agree to, balance shifts,
and every time you make an incorrect assumption,
balance shifts. In most scenarios, you can re-establish balance quickly with either a follow-up comment
or by changing the subject.

A further point: Don't associate balance-shifting
with negativity, because there are positive and negative shifts. The positive shifts are responsible for the
excitement in conversations. Often, with the appropriate response, negative balance shifts can work in
your favor; they may reveal someone's insecurity or
vulnerability.

Girl: no lol . . . im easy . . . hahahahahah

Remember, store all unusual smart aleck comments, such as "I'm easy," in your memory and, of
course, respond. But your response doesn't always
need to be sarcastic. In addition to responding, it's
also good just to react.

IM-er: no wayyy
Girl: i never make a guy work, if he thinks im worth it he'll
         make the effort
Girl: if not, he sees the door
Girl: im not easy in a sense like o its ok ill still give u
         regardless
IM-er: hahaha
IM-er: I would hope not
Girl: but im more of i appreciate u making the effort, i hope i
         can be as affectionate as u r

Vanessa has just re-established balance by thoroughly explaining something to me. If she wasn't
interested in the outcome of the conversation, she
wouldn't want to waste the energy explaining it, she
would just close the window.

Right after the girl reestablishes balance is a great
time to shift balance. When shifting immediately after a re-establishment, it's better to be on the soft
side with your delivery. Make it clear your jokes are
harmless.

IM-er: you made me work for your responding to my IM . . .
        believe this may have been attempt # 20 lol
Girl: thats not working though, i didnt make u do anything . . . u
        wanted to do it urself
IM-er: obviously
IM-er: but, you sure as hell gave me a challenge

Be prepared; most people will always deny their
game playing. If you decide to call them out on playing games, they will probably disregard your accusa-
tions and appear as though they have no idea what
you're talking about. People do that. When you get
caught in this situation, be prepared to act completely
nonchalant, even if it's not cool with you. Never show
your true reaction to a someone's initial game playing,
or you will lose. However, it's a good strategy to try on a
case-by-case basis, such as with Vanessa, because she
tempts you to give her a taste of her own medicine.

Girl: y do u say that
IM-er: I'm having some fun with you, that's all

A quick way to jump back to balance—right after blowing off a response with a playful "I'm having

some fun with you, that's all"—is to change the subject with a question.

IM-er: so, do you come to Manhattan often?
Girl: not as often as i wish :(
IM-er: what if you had a good reason . . . ?

Immediately after her response, follow up with a
cute question on the same subject, which really so-
lidifies the subject change. Now she is less likely to
remember what you were just talking about and, for
that matter, disagreeing about. It's easier to pull this
tactic off via IM than in an in-person conversation
because eye contact is very revealing.

Girl: then id def come lol

Balance is now re-established. After multiple
shifts in balance, you need a break. Vanessa and I
didn't actually fight, and we didn't even argue, but it
was an intense conversation. After a dialog like this,
you will feel heated, so the following portion of the
conversation is an effort to lighten the vibe. By now
you've already begun to understand how to communicate effectively with her and have a good idea of
how to maintain balance.

Girl: but its the time that i dont seem to have :(

After an intense discussion within a conversation, you
need time to cool off during a transitional period. You need
to take some time to smooth out intense energy and keep
communication relaxed for a bit.
    It's like a workout at the gym. For optimal results, it's
not recommended to stop right after you get your heart rate

up. To maximize your workout, you take a break and stretch after finishing cardio activity before moving to the next exercise, and, of course, you should finish with a good, relaxing stretch. To relate the gym logic to the context of an IM conversation: Don't end a conversation on an intense note. It's counterproductive because it is that last energy your potential match will associate with you.

My conversation with Vanessa continues in Chapter 3.

Chapter 3

Continuing with Vanessa:
Disarming Emotional Barriers

When continuing with Vanessa, it is important to try to lessen the intensity of the conversation. While some intensity is good, too much will likely make it difficult for you and/or your match to get comfortable. When we are comfortable enough to lower our guards, we become vulnerable, which allows others to see past our emotional barriers and get to know us.

More with Vanessa

IM-er: hmmm . . . well, would you make the time to get to know me?

Girl: depends r u worth the effort lol

In general, be prepared for a girl to be sarcastic

any time you ask her a corny question. Now that her guard is lowered, it's a good time to begin using her words whenever possible. Doing so will minimize her ability to challenge you. It is the best way to lighten the intensity of the discussion.

IM-er: well . . . according to your logic . . . I have def. made
        effort . . .
Girl: lol
IM-er: so, that's a good start
Girl: smart ass huh

She may be calling you a "smart ass," but she's not disagreeing. If name-calling like this upsets you, get over it quickly. Being uptight is not an attractive quality. This advice doesn't just apply to online dating; if you're easily offended by harmless teasing, banter or playfulness, you are going to have to get over it quickly, grow some thicker skin (psychologically . . . don't take everything literally) or, at the very least, make a concerted effort to mask your intolerance because it will most likely be a major turnoff to most people. Let playful comments roll off your shoulders. If someone is blatantly disrespectful, over-the-top obnoxious or just simply unpleasant, end your conversation and don't communicate further. It's way easier to avoid people when you don't see them in person.

IM-er: haha
IM-er: just keeping things interesting
Girl: make it more interesting by tellin me ur name lol
IM-er: sorry, thought I had done that about 20 times at this
        point :p
IM-er: lol
Im-er: My name is Keith

When your guard is down, it is important for you to maintain the same behavior or it may likely disturb the dynamic you have reached. For example, above she writes, "make it more interesting by tellin me ur name lol." She is being playful, which she has been throughout the conversation. To maintain the dynamic, I responded with consistent behavior: "sorry, thought I had done that about 20 times at this point :p" And then I follow up with "lol."

IM-er: I hope I've made you smile
IM-er: I'm still putting forth effort
IM-er: and regarding your question . . . . don't think you'd find a guy more worth the effort thank myself—depending on what you like, Vanessa
Girl: pleased to meet u –
IM-er: *not "thank"
IM-er: don't know where that came from
IM-er: *than
Girl: its ok, make sure it doesnt happen again in the future

With this kind of continuous banter, it's obvious that the balance is consistent at this point. She is coming to you with questions, such as pointing out that she doesn't know your name yet. It's expected she will make any sarcastic comments she can think of, simply because it's been her style throughout the conversation. But she isn't being a wiseass to be mean; clearly, if she's still talking to you, she's still interested.

IM-er: noted
Girl: so what --, do tell me what is it that u do
IM-er: I sell advertising
Girl: very nice :)

Girl: that explains ur vocabulary ;)
Girl: dont come across many ppl as intelligent as u

> If you read back through the conversation, you'll note I didn't use many "big" vocabulary words. As mentioned earlier in this conversation, when the girl opts to type lazily by slimming words down to one letter, it gives you the opportunity to do things differently too. If you choose to use proper grammar and spelling, it makes you seem more intelligent and confident.

IM-er: no . . . my vocabulary comes from being passionate about language
IM-er: and somehow maintaining some of my memory
IM-er: lol
Girl: very nice

> Here, Vanessa compliments me, but she assumes that my career path is responsible for my intelligence. This is an opportunity to talk myself up a bit. I don't necessarily agree with her assumptions. If you can correct a girl's assumptions about you, do so nicely and proudly, which makes you seem more complex and confident. It's never a good idea to opt to speak extensively about yourself, but when she brings up the topic, it's your chance to sell your greatest assets.

IM-er: I speak Spanish, Italian, and some French
Girl: oohhh trilingual i see
IM-er: well . . .
IM-er: tri-quat- lingual
IM-er: poly lingual
IM-er: lol

Girl: lol yea i meant to say polylingual hahahaha
IM-er: hahaha
IM-er: also
IM-er: I have a real estate license . . . but, not really using it
IM-er: and
IM-er: I'm a singer/songwriter
IM-er: I dabble a lot—lol
IM-er: yes . . . talking myself up here . . .
IM-er: gotta try to out-man my competition
Girl: nice life motto

As you can see, I took advantage of the opportunity to talk myself up, and you can too. But an exit strategy is needed because it will quickly become a major turn-off to keep myself as the main subject. Remember, people want to talk about themselves, so let them. It serves your benefit to let her talk about herself, because when you pay attention to what she tells you, she will reveal how to most effectively connect with her.

IM-er: so, going to be a physical therapist?
IM-er: and . . .
IM-er: you wonder why I assume you're sweet?

Now, I am changing the subject back to Vanessa, using information I gleaned from her profile.

Girl: hahah i can be a physical therapist with the worse bed side etiquette, it's happened before   lol
IM-er: hahaha
IM-er: well, if I were a patient, and I saw your face . . . . I'd be feeling better
Girl: if only my female patients would feel the same way
IM-er: some definitely will . . .

```
Girl:    lol
Girl:    very original
IM-er:   some will be eyeing you like a fat kid does cake
IM-er:   not as original
IM-er:   :p
Girl:    totally stealing my line!!!
```

After many sarcastic comments and much witty banter from Vanessa, her defenses seem to be fading. Eventually, even the toughest person gets tired of making constant argumentative commentary. In all cases, try to keep her smiling for as long as possible. Once you've established the energy, you have to maintain it. And, once you've managed to get her to lower her guard, you don't want to give her a chance or a reason to throw you any more curve balls. At this point, you want to continue the rapport while you begin inching toward your "close."

```
IM-er:   haha
IM-er:   so, what are you up to tonight?
```

This is a generic question I use to initiate the close of a conversation. I know that I want to get her number and finish the conversation soon. To be most effective, you don't want to lose the energy that you've already established. It's crucial that it's as close as possible to a mutual close, especially after a heated conversation.

The close happens when you're both ready to end the conversation at around the same time. It should feel like a natural conclusion; she shouldn't feel blown off. It is not necessarily important who initiates the close; what's important is that it feels natural and reciprocal.

Girl: well right now im working and doing laundry and then goin to a class at 8
IM-er: awwww
IM-er: I was thinking how enjoyable it'd be to talk to you on the phone . . .
Girl: lol I dont do phones not unless it's an emergency lol only text :)
IM-er: haha, hmmmm . . . well, then, I'll settle for texting
Girl: nice
IM-er: and, meeting you of course
IM-er: that is . . . if you feel I'm worth the effort . . . ?
Girl: hhmmm lets see how the texts goes, possibly

That was a good opportunity for me to use Vanessa's words, "worth the effort," to my favor. The only time that you ever want to use her words *against* her is to prevent her from playing hardball with you. In that circumstance, if you can use her own logic to prove the point that you are trying to make, it's much more difficult for her to disagree.

Further, when someone indicates they don't want to talk on the phone, it could be a red flag; not everyone likes to talk on the phone. Because communication is a crucial key to developing a relationship, it is important to connect with someone who can communicate effectively with you. I generally prefer never to limit myself to written communication unless it's the only option available; otherwise, more is likely to be lost in translation.

As a rule of thumb, always try to avoid being limited by means of communication. Don't confuse that to mean you should avoid limiting communication. You should not be in constant communication with your matches. Note that I wrote, ". . . try to avoid being limited by means of communication." That just

means it is far more effective to communicate using various forms of communication—phone, text, e-
mail, video chat—when possible.

IM-er: thought you were easy . . . :p
Girl: and u r totally gonna be picking on me with the effort
         comment huh
IM-er: hahaha, I'm going to do whatever it takes to meet you
IM-er: so
IM-er: if you just say . . . . "I'd like that" . . .
IM-er: then . . . .
IM-er: I'll lay off the effort commentary
Girl: lol

Don't forget, use her words against her when you
need to, such as, "thought you were easy . . ." It's a
great way to deal with someone who challenges you.

Girl: i want u to do whatever makes u happy ;)
IM-er: well, I want to meet you
IM-er: that would make me happy
IM-er: ;)
Girl: well if u play ur cardsd just right, that may happen ;)
IM-er: haha—I learn quickly
Girl: arent i just a lucky gal
IM-er: just play your cards right . . . and ...yess
IM-er: lol

You need to be persistent when dealing with a
girl like Vanessa. She will not make it easy for you to
succeed. Be prepared for at least one more challenge:
getting her phone number.

Girl: u got jokes huh lol
IM-er: I have wit

IM-er: remember, I am a songwriter
IM-er: if you want to hear . . . I can let you

When she is being sarcastic, try your best never to let her have the last word because, ultimately, that is how she controls the shift of balance. Toward the end of the conversation, you need to be able to maintain balance.

Girl: y do i feel like ull woo me pretty soon
Girl: haha
Girl: hahah*

Finally, Vanessa is showing some more vulnerability. In a sense she's telling me that I'm winning; she's admitting that I have the capability to "woo" her. In doing so, she's giving me the ability to shift the conversational balance. The person who can shift the balance controls it. Now I'm controlling the balance, and it's important to maintain control so I can sustain social balance. It's not a good idea to be sarcastic when you're focusing on balance at the end of a conversation. Just be fun and genuine.

IM-er: cause I'm goal-oriented and...
IM-er: I'm an achiever
Girl: and get what u want by the end of the day huh lol

She is giving me the credit I deserve. Since I'm not trying to take advantage of the situation, she isn't making it difficult to maintain the balance. This is the way you should keep it. Now it can be a smooth ending.

IM-er: I'll only woo you if you want to be wooed
IM-er: but
IM-er: hmmm . . . .
IM-er: I'm going to leave that at, "but"
IM-er: lol

Right before your transition to getting her phone number, it's good to keep up the playful banter. This makes it less likely she will second guess her decision to give you her number. She will think, *What's the harm in giving this fun guy my number?* That is exactly what you want her to think, and it's the result of consistent, positive energy.

Girl: lol
IM-er: haha
IM-er: would you like to hear some of my tunes?
Girl: eventually, i wouldnt mind ;)
IM-er: afraid you'll be easily wooed?
IM-er: lol
Girl: yea cuz im a sucker for chick flicks and im oozing with sweetness lol

She's being a wiseass again and using my words against me. What a surprise.

IM-er: hahahaha
IM-er: in any case, you're really adorable to my standards
IM-er: and you've got some spice
IM-er: and, I'm a liking it
IM-er: lol
IM-er: we skipped over exchanging numbers . . . . let's do that
IM-er: mine's ###-###-####
Girl: lol
Girl: ###-###-####

If you're going for the phone number right after she makes a wiseass remark, just ignore the comment. It's better to respond with a random, genuine compliment and then suggest, "Let's exchange numbers." No question, just a suggestion. It's more difficult to say "no" to a suggestion than to a question.

Now that you've gotten her number, it's all easy from here. Just be sure not to get too comfortable so you don't sabotage your previous efforts.

<<<<<<< An Extended Pause >>>>>>>

IM-er: did you take a grocery shopping break?
IM-er: lol
Girl: hahaha sorry
Girl: phone call from mama, shes in paris right now
IM-er: ahhh
IM-er: Paris
IM-er: trop belle
Girl: im guessing u said very beautiful in french?
IM-er: close . . . . "too beautiful"
IM-er: I give you an A for attempt ;)
Girl: sad, i forgot how to speak french :(
Girl: took the language for abt 4 years
IM-er: you're a smarty . . . you can re-learn
IM-er: I haven't really practiced spanish or italian in 6 years, guess I'm lucky I didn't forget
Girl: lol i took the language from 1-5 grade, lol doubt i remember anything
Girl: lol
IM-er: haha
IM-er: it's ok
Girl: but thanks for the vote of confdience!

If you want to continue the conversation after getting the phone number, make sure you keep up your energy and continue to keep her guard down. Ultimately, you want her to feel she made a good decision in giving you her number. The easiest way to do that is to make her feel good about herself while you continue chatting.

IM-er: you have many wonderful assets, I assure you, Vanessa
IM-er: I'll give you multiple votes
IM-er: but, only if it assists the wooing
IM-er: lol
Girl: hahahaa
IM-er: yea, so, smart move not listening to my tunes
IM-er: :p
IM-er: you'd just . . . .. melt
Girl: oh oh oh, cocky tonight arent we
IM-er: hahaha
IM-er: nah, had to mix it up for you
IM-er: but
IM-er: certainly confident
IM-er: it was more along the lines of . . . . wishful thinking
IM-er: haha

If you have the nerve to make a cocky comment after getting her phone number, it's best to follow it up with a self-deprecating joke. That allows you to seem genuine and honest, and it will soften the blow of your cocky comment.

Girl: lol
Girl: at least ure honest
IM-er: yes, I am
IM-er: although, I will be honest an say I am VERY proud of

IM-er: the music I've written
IM-er: *and
Girl: what kind of music do u write
IM-er: all different kinds . . . but, my default genre is singer/ songwriter pop/rock . . . right w/i the realm of old school John Mayer, minus the over-the-top ego

Preferably, you want to try to switch the subject matter away from yourself whenever possible. Also, if you are going to bash someone else, try to do so in a clever fashion; otherwise, you will seem angry or worse, jealous.

Girl: nice choice of words
IM-er: haha, thought you'd like that
IM-er: being fecitious, or, did you like my choice of words?
Girl: being what?
Girl: lol
IM-er: *facetious
IM-er: shame on you . . . making me check spelling w/ google
IM-er: lol

If a girl is going to call you out for misspelling, then you have to make a comeback. The worst part in this situation is that Vanessa was right, I did misspell, but more than likely, she knew what I meant. So, even in the end, the challenge is never completely over. Making a further joke of the situation is the best way to respond.

Girl: shame on u for mispelling!
Girl: lol

Ironically, she misspelled *misspelling*, but there's no need to overdo criticism. Don't go out of your way to create friction when you're on a mission.

IM-er: haha
IM-er: can't WAIT till I catch you
IM-er: hahahaha
IM-er: I WILL make the effort
IM-er: lol
Girl: be gentle if u catch me, for i am very fragile:(
Girl: :(

As soon as I jumped back with a defense, Vanessa showed more vulnerability. When a girl uses an adjective similar to *sensitive*, she is telling you, "Hey, I'm vulnerable, and I'm just playing around with you, so take it easy." If a girl as challenging as Vanessa shows vulnerability, you've won. If you create enough context to allow her to show some sensitivity, you should acknowledge it and try to make her smile.

IM-er: goodness . . . it's really just not fair for any girl to be as freaking adorable as you are
IM-er: now you're fragile too?
Girl: of course i am lol
IM-er: sweet, sensitive and fragile . . .
Girl: lethal combo huh
IM-er: you're my quintessential type
Girl: u double checked that word didnt ya lol
IM-er: you'll be my lil Humpty Dumpty, but I assure you . . . I won't let you sit on any high ledges

It's always a good idea to use metaphors if possible, especially if you're trying to be cute. In addition to its literary value, it will make you seem more intelligent and witty.

IM-er: hahaha
IM-er: yes

IM-er: I did
IM-er: google, up front and ready
IM-er: but
IM-er: proudly, I was correct on my first attempt
Girl: very nice!
IM-er: haha
Girl: so how do u feel abt learning Hebrew?
IM-er: actually . . .
IM-er: I was going to last summer
IM-er: began teaching myself
IM-er: not too brutal . . . just didn't have much time
IM-er: then
IM-er: I met my ex . . .
IM-er: I looooove learning languages
IM-er: but, at this point . . .
Girl: so maybe ill teach u, cause lo and behold i am from Israel after all :)
IM-er: when it comes to Hebrew . . .
IM-er: ani yachol medeber ivrit
Girl: hahahahahah
IM-er: unfortunately, didn't learn enough that week
IM-er: ani lo medeber ivrit
Girl: u can always learn
IM-er: ep
IM-er: *yep
IM-er: most definitely
Girl: u still got time, esp before meeting me ;)
IM-er: haha
IM-er: that's a whole lotta effort just to woo
IM-er: haha

This is the very end of the conversation. At this point I've succeeded. She's given me her number and wants to meet. It's good to end with a positive balance shift. It's okay to make a fun, sarcastic comment with a girl like Vanessa, because you know she will come back at you with the same, which is your goal. Energy given should yield energy returned.

Girl: aawww someone is afraid of a challenge ;)
IM-er: ummmm . . . learning the Hebrew language might just take a little bit of time
IM-er: haha
IM-er: cut me some slack
Girl: hahahaah
Girl: fine, ill cut us ome slack ;)

Balance is now established, so we continue with the shifting and let the energy flow until the last line. At that point, you'll be tired; I was. I exerted a ton of mental energy throughout the conversation. When you encounter a situation like this, you should exit sooner than later. It's crucial you avoid the point where you can no longer continue, are too tired to keep up or no longer want to exert the energy.

On a related note, typos happen from time to time, but you should try to minimize them because:

· If you don't correct yourself, a typo can change the meaning of the word, sentence, question, statement or more. Your words may be interpreted as you not knowing your typo was a mistake and, as a result, your intelligence may be questioned. It could also be interpreted as laziness, which can be a major turn-off.

· When you immediately correct yourself, which I recommend, you may unintentionally interrupt the flow of dialog or a change in subject, both of which can lead to the loss of energy.

IM-er: what?

IM-er: :p

Girl: cut u*

IM-er: hahaha

Girl: sounded even worse lol

IM-er: yea . . . . but, as long as you use the butter knife . . . I'll
        survive longer

Girl: lucky u, i have no idea where my butter knife is lol

IM-er: I have no witty response for that

Girl: is that good or bad

IM-er: haha, just honest

IM-er: I mean . . . I've been on a roll

Girl: all good things come to an end huh

At this point, I've created context for a social
foundation but need to keep up with her until the last
line. As I mentioned earlier, the energy you end with
is the energy by which you'll be remembered.

IM-er: no . . .

IM-er: just momentarily

IM-er: my determination outweighs my exhaustion

IM-er: I'm as perseverant as they come

Girl: very nice nice

IM-er: so, what are you passionate about?

This is a great question to ask a girl, but always
make sure when asking a question like "What are your
passions?" to be prepared to answer the question in return. Although, in the best case scenario, this question
should be asked much earlier in the conversation.

Girl: o wow its been so long since ive been passionate abt
        anything lol

Girl: ive been so locked up in my room and school's library

that i forgot where my passions lie
IM-er: where did they used to lie?
IM-er: *lay
IM-er: I copied your mistake there :p
IM-er: actually
IM-er: no
IM-er: it is lie
IM-er: wow . . . just gave you major fuel in pointing out more mistakes
IM-er: lol
Girl: lol
Girl: Keith, im so sorry but i have to go now u have my number so def text me and we'll chat later k

This is the ending you want; the girl has to go but reminds you that she wants to hear from you. You're golden!

Girl: it was a pleasure speaking with u tonight, hope to hear from you soon

<<<<<<< IM Conversation Ended >>>>>>>

As mentioned previously, my conversation with Vanessa was a rare circumstance. While many people may challenge you at different points in your conversations, most will not battle you to the extent that Vanessa did with me. This example is important to help familiarize you with different response tactics to use during balance shifts because conversations can quickly move in so many different directions.

In the end, Vanessa and I texted back and forth a lot; in fact, that's all we did. While our banter continued in our text messages, and I am certainly a patient person, a couple of weeks was generally the time limit I set for myself to meet a new match. If it didn't happen within that time frame, I would move on to connect with new matches, which is eventually what happened with Vanessa.

Chapter 4

Conversation with Andrea:
Establishing Levels of Balance

While Vanessa challenged me with constant shifts in balance, Andrea brings much intense energy. This conversation presents *energy triggers*, which can offset a *trigger effect*. In this chapter, you will become familiar with energy triggers and understand how they can lead to a trigger effect, a cycle of intense energy that is initiated by an energy trigger.

An energy trigger is an emotionally intense comment or statement that exposes someone's vulnerability and is intended to elicit a response. For example, saying, "I love you," is an energy trigger that is generally intended to elicit the response, "I love you too." The reciprocation of "I love you," while wonderful, is only appropriate in a scenario with mature emotional context. I would certainly not advise saying the phrase any time during early communications.

You cannot prevent someone else's energy triggers;

however, by understanding what offsets a trigger effect, and of course, knowing its consequences, you may be able to minimize the intensity of a conversation.

IM-ing with Andrea

IM-er: hi there

<<<<<<< Waiting to Connect >>>>>>>

<<<<<<< Connected >>>>>>>

Girl: Hi :)
Girl: How are you?
IM-er: glad to connect w/you
IM-er: I'm Keith

I opened with "glad to connect w/you" because it's not aggressive, yet it's warm and soft, which gives it a genuine vibe.

Prior to this conversation, Andrea had used a dating website tool to let me know that she was intrigued by my profile. Such tools, when available, may vary in name and functionality. She also used a website tool to indicate that she felt we would be compatible. Given the number of online dating websites from which to choose, you may find that while some offer various useful tools, others may not be so helpful. It's all based on your personal preferences. It is very beneficial to become comfortable and efficient with any tools provided by the site(s) you choose to use.

Girl: I'm Andrea. It's nice to meet you despite it being online
IM-er: you too!

Girl: thx
IM-er: I have to be forthright with you . . .

     Generally, writing, "I have to be forthright with you
. . ." is a good strategy because it sounds even more
genuine than "I have to be honest with you . . ." "Forthright" is a more formal word choice than "honest,"
not that there's anything wrong with using the word
"honest." Remember, these aren't rules by which I
restricted myself, these are just examples of different strategies and my reasoning for a dynamic selection of words. So you can say "honest"; in fact, I did,
from time to time, I didn't this time because I preferred to begin the conversation more formally with
"forthright." Within the context of a casual conversation, using less common expressions and formal
word choices will help you differentiate yourself from
the competition. Word choice and delivery is crucial.
In an IM conversation, almost every detail of written
words makes a big difference.

IM-er: you're 5'8, does it bother you that I'm really 5'7?
IM-er: my profile says 5'8
IM-er: I rounded up an inch, so sue me
IM-er: lol

     When you opt to tell a girl something that may be
a turn-off, be prepared with a follow-up joke. Men will
often lie about their height when online dating, but
don't be stupid about it. Do you really think you'll get
away with a few extra inches? You probably won't.
An inch is okay, possibly two, but anything more is
pushing it. So, it's a good idea to find a way to tell the
truth before your first meeting.

Girl: depends if you can make me laugh
Girl: I'll sue
Girl: haha
Girl: nbd
IM-er: so . . .
IM-er: not really then, huh
Girl: I have to be forthright with you
Girl: I am only 5ft 7 and 3/4
Girl: lol
Girl: I do prefer a taller man though

Thus far, I can already tell that this girl likes to be communicative. She has already begun copying my word choice, which is an immediate sign that she is involving herself in the conversation with minimal balance. I consider this minimal balance because while it is very early in the conversation, we had already reached the point of mutual active engagement. But she's already throwing me a slight curve ball by telling me that she prefers someone taller.

If you encounter a similar curve ball, an easy, workable course of action is to intrigue her with words.

IM-er: I was afraid you were going to say 5'9
Girl: ha
IM-er: well, can't be what i'm not
IM-er: but, I am a lot of great things
Girl: I think you are being a bit superficial
IM-er: how so?
Girl: not just your height matters silly

She now has established the first balance shift, "I think you are being a bit superficial," but immediately re-establishes the balance, "not just your height matters silly." This immediate reestablishment of energy indicates chemistry. When a girl throws the word "superficial" at you, be prepared to defend yourself; it is not a good word to associate with you, especially via IM. It's a hassle to be associated in a negative way via IM; it will be more challenging to change her perspective through written dialog, which can cause it to be more problematic.

IM-er: of course
Girl: interesting way to greet someone
IM-er: Just wanted to be honest with you before I lay it on thick :p
Girl: oh nooo . . . I'm not sure you can . . . I need a true romantic not a farce

See, it's also okay to use the word "honest" from time to time.

Now Andrea is starting to seem like what I refer to as a "brat." She already threw "superficial" at me, and now she's critiquing my greeting style. When I try to come back with a cute comment, she feels the need to say, "I'm not sure you can . . . I need a true romantic not a farce."

Well, now it's officially on. She's telling me what she wants. She wants romantic, so I'm going to be romantic! Flip on the switch and don't turn back! Keep in mind, though, after she says, "I'm not sure you can . . . I need a true romantic not a farce," this is a blatant challenge—and very early in the conversation. In this case, you should anticipate that she is likely going to be challenging throughout the entire conversation.

IM-er: I epitomize romantic

Girl: feel free to try.
Girl: jk
IM-er: did you read my profile
IM-er: ?
Girl: I liked your screenname . . . lol
Girl: yes
IM-er: so, then you'd believe that I'm a romantic
Girl: there are many capitalized words which seems bossy
IM-er: haha
IM-er: interesting
IM-er: you're a tough cookie, huh

Now she's attacking my writing style, which I definitely do not appreciate; but, unfortunately, you never want to show too much emotion in the initial stage of an IM conversation—you will seem crazy. Don't react, just counteract. Bring on a strong verbal defense.

Girl: italics are cool but you really really were screaming
Girl: ha

She's continuing to judge the writing style in my profile. And, websites don't necessarily give you the option to play around with font and style; in fact, I did not have the option to use italics in my profile. I wouldn't have been wrong to write back, "Okay, and you're acting quite judgmental," but that, of course, would be counterproductive if I were trying to establish rapport. You don't want to have to offset a negative balance shift this early in the conversation.

IM-er: haha
Girl: no
IM-er: I was being passionate
Girl: just playing

Girl: ok . . .
Girl: I like that

    Yes! Passion is almost always a good thing. A woman who is looking for a relationship will appreciate a man with passion. If you can ever get away with excusing something as passion, do it. Believe me, it will definitely not work in every circumstance, but it's a great rationalization. Remember, as is common to many situations in this book, a great way to avoid further attack is to change the subject back to her. The more she reveals about herself, the better prepared you are to avoid negative judgments and reestablish balance during a shift. The expression, "Know thine enemy," is appropriate here. Obviously, though, the girl you're trying to win over is not your enemy, so your best strategy is to "Know thine potential match."

IM-er: seriously . . . you have a perfect profile
Girl: thank you
Girl: that is sweet
IM-er: like . . . literally. I kinda melted in a masculine way, just
         from reading it
IM-er: lol

    Now you've re-established balance simply by changing the subject. Most people would prefer to talk about themselves rather than give you a hard time. Notice how I changed the subject back to Andrea; I quickly followed-up with a personalized compliment (referring to her profile).

Girl: It needs editing but I gave up and just kept it simple
         after realizing there is no such thing as perfect

```
        especially in a silly online bio
Girl:   awwww
Girl:   you are sweet
Girl:   hehe
IM-er:  I am
IM-er:  indeed
IM-er:  like I said . . . a lot of good things
IM-er:  lol
```

When girls like Andrea decide to argue with your compliments, just ignore it. Never feed a person's need to fish for extra compliments during an IM conversation. If you feed into that type of demand, you fall into a trap: The person will continue to take and give nothing in return. If that is the case, you may end up with only an e-mail address—and never get a response. And, even if you did get her number and had the opportunity to go on a date, what are you looking for? A non-reciprocal relationship?

```
Girl:   I'm 29 not 28
IM-er:  importatn question though
IM-er:  *important . . .
Girl:   did you see?
IM-er:  is kosher important to you . . . .
IM-er:  I mean
IM-er:  do you care that I eat pork and shellfish?
Girl:   I look 23 though . . . its confusing . . . bc I'm so healthy
        and work out
Girl:   eat whatever you like
Girl:   I'm a vegetarian
IM-er:  you're lovely
Girl:   why is that important?
```

At this point in the conversation, you can already

tell that Andrea is extremely self-conscious. I didn't ask her about her age, and I didn't mention anything about how young she looks prior to my writing, "you're lovely"; yet, she hints that she wants a physical compliment by writing, "I look 23 though..." See how she generally doesn't acknowledge physical compliments? This should be a hint that she likes to stroke her own ego about her appearance and prefers to receive personality-related compliments.

IM-er: a vegetarian, huh?
Girl: i love sushi
Girl: not VEGAN, VEGETARIAN..
Girl: haha
Girl: passionate
IM-er: I mean . . . I don't have a problem with it . . . I just hope your cool being around meat, often

If you bring something up, it's imperative to explain your thought. It's not a good idea to bring up something and then say, "Never mind." Doing so will make you seem less confident. A lack of confidence can be a major turnoff. Once you reveal insecurities via IM, it is nearly impossible to recover. Do not confuse insecurities with vulnerabilities. *Vulnerability* can be described as someone's exposure of personal emotions and feelings to others. People are often reluctant to expose their vulnerabilities, which is healthy and normal, because we're naturally hard wired to protect ourselves. While vulnerability is a natural, protective instinct, *insecurity* is the display of a person's lack of confidence. Revealing your own vulnerabilities will be helpful in getting someone else to do the same.

Girl: spelling
IM-er: you're
Girl: ummm. I could care less what you eat
Girl: wow
Girl: who have you dated?

Obviously, Andrea's being sarcastic about my single spelling error and bringing up that I eat meat, and what she's insinuating is that I have dated abnormal women who judge me for what I eat. Consequently, what she is really saying is, "I'm not like the other women you have dated . . . I'm special . . . I'm cool . . . I'm sweet . . . me, me, me, I, I, I." Despite the fact that she isn't directly speaking about herself, she is most certainly indirectly doing so. Ultimately, she is asking me to recognize how special and wonderful she is, and she wants me to compliment her.

IM-er: don't ask
IM-er: lol
Girl: such silly questions
IM-er: don't ask . . .
Girl: I've never heard of being judged by such superficial nonsense

Really? In what century and country is this girl living in? I thought to myself.

Girl: just wow
Girl: k
Girl: you should be happy in life
Girl: :)

Once again, Andrea continues making comments, using words like "silly" and "superficial," intended to remind me what she feels does not define her. These are the types of insecurities you shouldn't feed into, so don't ask for her opinions regarding things that bother her. She will likely go on and on about her pet peeves, which won't be much fun for you. Also, if you encourage her to think of her pet peeves, she will get annoyed. When you evoke negative emotions, it will likely hinder your success.

IM-er: I love your outlook
IM-er: where in Connecticut do you live?
Girl: thx
Girl: ha . . . Greenwhich . . . just completed grad school in June and got a job here after the boards . . .

I assumed she meant Greenwich, but who's keeping track of misspellings.

IM-er: btw, Andrea is a beautiful name :)
IM-er: what's your fav flower/color?

These are some of my favorite types of questions. A theory of mine, which I refer to as the *Association Theory*, holds that discussing topics someone associates with pleasure, you can influence the mood shift—essentially Pavlov's theory. But the topic change has to be as smooth and subtle as possible. I gave a good example just now when we were discussing where we live in relation to one another, then I gave a random compliment—not about aesthetics—and asked a specific, personal-preference question about flowers. It's pretty rare for a girl not to like flowers, so for her to think about flowers is likely to trigger a positive thought.

Girl: I like tropical flowers and pink or purple fave colors . . .
         oh and sea foam
IM-er: favorite eye color?
Girl: on a guy?
IM-er: yes
Girl: green
IM-er: sorry, mine are blue :p
IM-er: very blue
Girl: it matters more what is behind the eyes
Girl: me 2
IM-er: indeed
IM-er: I know
IM-er: honestly . . . aesthetically, you're very . . . . wow

It's important to establish a connection via IM. You don't necessarily have to get someone to say that she finds you attractive. Obviously, if she's talking to you, she is expressing some basic interest, but receiving a compliment is important because it indicates a stronger balance and engagement.

Balance isn't just based on maintaining a good flow, it's based on a mutual understanding that you're both on a similar page regarding interest level.

Girl: but mine turn green depending on what I wear . . . idky
         but I like it
Girl: thank you
Girl: as are you
IM-er: well, thank you
Girl: you are very welcome

A stronger balance is now established.

IM-er: I'm not used to a girl reciprocating compliments like
         that

Girl: why?
IM-er: don't know
IM-er: women generally looove to play games
Girl: how long have you lived in Manhattan that you are
         meeting such cold people?

Again, she ignores my indirect compliments about our positive rapport, the mutual exchange of compliments.

IM-er: haha
Girl: seriously
IM-er: my whole life that's what I've had the luxury of finding
Girl: same
IM-er: which is why I'm still single
IM-er: I don't like casual bs anymore
Girl: I'm single because I am very very picky
IM-er: just isn't fulfilling
Girl: and particular
Girl: its lame
IM-er: haha
Girl: never got into that so much
IM-er: agreed
IM-er: so, a straight forward girl, huh
IM-er: I dig
Girl: but the offers are ridiculous that I get asked
IM-er: I dig a lot
IM-er: what offers?
Girl: well . . . I am sure I play games if you end up doing that
         but I tend to just write off a guy who does that into the
         category of "never call"
Girl: ever
Girl: y
Girl: jk
IM-er: haha

IM-er: what are you doing for the rest of the night?

Here she goes again, but she makes a loaded statement when she writes, "but the offers are ridiculous that I get asked," which is ultimately an indirect request for me to ask her to elaborate. There are two options in this scenario: 1) change the subject or 2) ask her to elaborate. Unfortunately, asking her to elaborate is the most effective way to maintain balance, so occasionally I have to ask.

Be sure, if she begins going off on a tangent, you change the subject before she has the chance to elaborate too much; elaborations are rarely short and sweet. You can't ignore a topic that continues to resurface. But once you've given her any opportunity to vent or explain, the next time she wants to, you can casually say something like "right . . . you were telling me . . ." This respectfully halts her soliloquy before it begins, enabling your subject change.

So, it's no secret that Andrea can be quite annoying. And, honestly, if she hadn't been really attractive in her pictures, I probably wouldn't have made the exception to continue our conversation considering the constant challenges and self-conscious comments. This created a frustrating social dynamic.

But none of us is perfect. Yes, I was being shallow to an extent, but in all fairness, she did seem like a nice person, was really attractive and was most certainly not boring. Keep in mind that people sometimes get nervous, and when nervous, they may act a bit out of character.

As I recommended earlier, you should keep an open mind. Your greatest match may be having an off day during your first communication, so don't be too quick to write off a potential match just because they make you work for their affection and keep their attention. Personally, I happen to admire a good challenge; "easy" doesn't keep me interested.

Girl: just some guys are very stupid and forget a beautiful woman can have an IQ
Girl: lol . . . ummm . . . my IQ is clearly not reflected well in this spelling
Girl: lol

Again, she is indirectly begging me to recognize that she is smart, special and more than just a beautiful girl, blah, blah, blah. Again, try to ignore it as frequently as possible or she will continue to request and expect it.

IM-er: I want to give you a call in like an hour
Girl: I will be going to the gym soon
IM-er: yea, I was going to go do some weights too
IM-er: and shower
Girl: and I really don't just give out my number right away
IM-er: well, I have to be forthright again
Girl: ?
IM-er: I get good vibes from you

This is one of my favorite words, as you have already read. "Vibes" is a great word to use via IM. It sounds confident and genuine and not nearly as common as it was years ago. Every differentiation helps you stand out from the crowd.

Girl: hehe
Girl: I am getting the same from you

A strong balance is established. If she reciprocates that

sentiment, theoretically, you're golden and should get the phone number. Once you have reached that point, it's critical to base your following words on her preceding demeanor. You should know what will set her off negatively and avoid it. And, of course, you should know what pushes her in the right direction, so, focus on that.

If you disrupt the vibe you've now established, it can still collapse. It's a delicate situation, because if a girl has decided that she gets a good vibe from you, she has decided to trust her gut instinct about you. If you give her a reason to second-guess that decision, you will almost definitely not succeed.

IM-er: Cool. So let's be spontaneous
Girl: could be the pic if black and white cropped photoshop . . . what are you looking at?

I was suggesting the option of using an audio/ video feature within the IM.

Andrea is referring to one of my profile pictures; it was black and white.

Girl: of
IM-er: all of your pics
Girl: lol . . . no in your profile pic . . . what are you glancing at?
IM-er: I can let you see me, now, but I'm in gym clothes

I was suggesting the option of using an audio/ video feature within the IM.

IM-er: oh
IM-er: lol
IM-er: nevermind
IM-er: it was a headshot . . . a friend took it
Girl: last person I asked told me himself . . . ha

```
IM-er:  I hate the way I look in still frame
Girl:   k
Girl:   I feel like you could write a beautiful poem
IM-er:  I write beautiful music
IM-er:  :)
Girl:   even better
IM-er:  if I don't say so myself
Girl:   ha
Girl:   you are slightly biased
Girl:   jk
IM-er:  well . . . I base it on success
```

This is my loaded statement: My goal is to lead her to ask me to elaborate.

```
IM-er:  lol
Girl:   how so? success how?
```

If you want to flaunt an achievement for your ego's benefit, don't just say it casually; you must convey it modestly. Be vague, yet intrigue her to ask you to clarify. Once she asks you specifically, then it won't seem as though you are self-promoting, but you will still come off as impressive.

```
IM-er:  some awards I achieved in the past
Girl:   such as?
IM-er:  4 runner-ups in VH1's song of the year, intl contest
IM-er:  pop genre
Girl:   p.s. you are the 1st profile with all the details I like . . .
        even down to the tv shows but dexter creeps me out a
        bit
Girl:   WOW
IM-er:  haha
Girl:   congratulations!
```

If you get the praise that you wanted, change the subject. It's horribly unattractive for anyone to boast.

IM-er: it's usually a great show
IM-er: I'm all about new tv shows
Girl: did you see Archer?
IM-er: not familiar
Girl: omg . . . over the top . . . youtube it . . . funny cartoon
         with like dark humor
Girl: its funny
Girl: dry humor
IM-er: lol
IM-er: cool
IM-er: will do
Girl: I thought I'd hate it but its funny. I was very very wrong
Girl: what else would you like to share or ask?
Girl: and btw . . . I get that good feeling from talking to you
         so thx for just being you

This is a great example of an energy trigger. It feels great to be told ". . . thanks for being you." But do you really want someone who you haven't already met to say such intense things to you? It certainly intensifies the conversational energy, but it's problematic because you may need to reciprocate the comment to maintain balance. Doing so can lead to an ongoing cycle of intense energy, which I refer to as the trigger effect, because once this cycle begins, there is no turning back—it will only continue to intensify.

I have broken the conversation with Andrea into two chapters. This chapter addressed effective strategies to establish increasingly stronger levels of balance with a challenging match. Chapter 5 focuses on how to control and maintain balance within conversations that present intense levels of energy.

Chapter 5

Conversation with Andrea, Continued:
Controlling Energy Flows

Throughout the conversation with Andrea, you may have likely become increasingly baffled by my willingness to continue the dialog. Well, the energy becomes even more intense. Yes, she said something sweet, "so thx for just being you," but along with what is extremely sweet comes intense energy.

If you aren't interested, you might want to cut your losses when red flags arise at the early stages of conversation. That is by no means a hard and fast rule, just some friendly advice and something to keep in mind. Of course, every circumstance has its unique details, and there can certainly be exceptions. Please keep in mind, however, that most people are taught to try to make good first impressions, especially in the dating process. If you want your potential match to like you, avoid turning them off before they have a chance to develop feelings for you. Once they have, they will be more tolerant of your potentially less appealing qualities. Having said that, when there is a red flag (or red flags) during the initial stages, just be leery; it could likely get worse going forward.

IM-er: honestly, I'm excited about the idea of matching a voice to this vibe

This is a subtle attempt to reinforce that I want her number. If she has no intention to give me her number, she will likely respond one of two ways: either she will ignore my attempt or will indicate she is uncomfortable.

Girl: agreed
IM-er: wow, that's the sweetest thing a girl has ever written to me

Here, I'm referring to when she just wrote, "so thx for just being you," at the end of Chapter 4.

Girl: good things come to those who wait
Girl: ha
Girl: jk
IM-er: right back at you, Andrea
IM-er: you're extraordinarily communicative
Girl: really..I am spontaneous . . . but I have to be cautious bc there are some oddballs on this site
Girl: yes, I am
IM-er: well, take a leap of faith
Girl: this is why Im able to help my clients

If she responds to your attempt but procrastinates on the number exchange, it's better to play it cool. You can be cute about it and make it obvious without demanding it. You also have to space out your attempts. You can't ask multiple times in a row or else it will disrupt the balance, and worse, it will make you seem desperate, which is very unattractive. If she continues to put off the number exchange, you have to be prepared to call her out on it.

Don't be afraid of rejection. What do you really have to lose other than your time? Remember, the greatest benefits of using IM are it's easier to deal with rejection, if it occurs, and you can maximize your chances of avoiding it by carefully selecting your comments.

IM-er: p p pa pawease
IM-er: lol

It's okay to make a joke like this, "p p pa pawease," as long as you're making it clear that you're really not desperate, hence my adding "lol."

Girl: communication is the key component to developing in every regard
Girl: ha
Girl: trust me . . . I was naive in the past . . . thought everyone is a good person and then realized I was wrong . . . however I still really think that inside
Girl: so I am playing tough here but really its bc we r meeting online

If the girl makes a comment like, "so I am playing tough here but really its bc we r meeting online," then she's giving you an incentive to ask. She's indirectly telling you that she's purposely challenging you. In this scenario you shouldn't be afraid to ask for her number. For the record, you should *never* be afraid to ask; in fact, the only thing you should fear is the consequence of *not* asking.

IM-er: I'm extremely picky, but have a really good feeling about you
IM-er: better than I'm used to

Reassurance is a good way to reinforce her comfort in giving you her number. You can remind her that you're really intrigued by her. Making her feel good will make her more comfortable with you, and she therefore will be less hesitant to give you her number.

Girl: and many guys say that to me
Girl: but thank you
Girl: I actually believe you
Girl: you seem rare and exquisite
Girl: like fine wine. Ha
IM-er: something about you is ridiculously inviting
Girl: hehe
Girl: thx
IM-er: wow, don't know who lays it on thicker now
IM-er: lol
Girl: its bc I like you silly
Girl: I do
Girl: ha
IM-er: well, I like talking to you too, Andrea
Girl: but we'll see . . . I can always be wrong
Girl: awww
Girl: thx
Girl: so are you :)
IM-er: wow
IM-er: I could get used to this
IM-er: for sure

Girl: ?
Girl: what?
IM-er: communication and reciprocity
IM-er: our rapport
Girl: you have met way way too many cold people
IM-er: you're so sweet and verbally affectionate
Girl: I'm just normal and kind

If you're going to lay it on thick, then lay it on *thick*. Try to be original. You don't need to make up expressions, but it always seems more genuine when you word things differently than she is used to. Again, do not copy me. It doesn't hurt me if you copy my words, it hurts you in the long run if you try to be someone you are not, because 1) It's not genuinely you and 2) if they like it, they like my words, not yours. Your goal should be for your matches to like you, not me.

IM-er: no
IM-er: sweetness and verbal affection is not normal
IM-er: but, it's great :)
Girl: well, you deserve it...you seem to have taken time to express yourself in your profile and I appreciate that
Girl: hehe
Girl: and just to clarify: haha is laugh and hehe is the crush laugh
Girl: ha
Girl: now I'm amused I typed that
IM-er: :)
Girl: sp*
Girl: so I gg
Girl: doing taxes b4 the gym
Girl: yay
IM-er: I really want to talk to you tonight

IM-er: like, a lot

> Now a sufficient amount of time has elapsed be-
> tween attempts for her number. When spacing out
> attempts, it's crucial that you don't lay it on too thick
> the first time, or else your subesquent attempts won't
> be *nearly* as effective.

Girl: why?
IM-er: the thought just excites me

> At this point, she doesn't really need to know
> why, but she's asking because she is fishing for reas-
> surance. So reassure her.

Girl: why?
IM-er: kinda feel like I'm back in middle school
Girl: lol
IM-er: butterflies and corny shit
Girl: why does everyone say that?????
Girl: omg
IM-er: which?
Girl: I remind people of being younger apparently
Girl: idky

> *OMG!* I thought, *This girl needs to stop with the
> me, me, me, I, I, I.*

IM-er: no
IM-er: I mean...
IM-er: the excitement, the rush
IM-er: the banter

> This "the excitement, the rush . . . the banter" is
> what I refer to as the triple entendre. Since a double

entendre is when a particular wording has a double meaning, I refer to this tactic as a triple entendre—not insinuating that it has a triple meaning, but because the delivery intensifies the words' effect. It is very powerful and effective, especially when you're laying it on thick. A triple entendre isn't three compliments; rather, it is dissecting one compliment into two parts. The first part uses two formal descriptors to encapsulate the emotional element, formally acknowledging the descriptor with "the," such as when I said, "the excitement" and "the rush," followed by a formal term to describe the element of focus, such as when I referred to the quality of our dialog as "the banter."

Girl: awwwwwwww
Girl: you r cute times 10

The triple entendre can be very effective and can help generate a ricochet effect because it can resonate; it seems poetic.

IM-er: well, I just want your number x 1
IM-er: lol
Girl: ha
IM-er: I'm not being greedy
Girl: nope
IM-er: how about just taking a chance on a sweet, genuine guy . . .
IM-er: what's the worst that could really happen?
Girl: tanti bacci
IM-er: grazie bella
Girl: now, is that what u say to a friend or like a child?
Girl: idk
Girl: that is all the italian I know

Girl: I know some Greek

     Now she is blatantly ignoring my request for her number—it's time to call her out on it. Once you've begun to take this route, you need to be firm with your request.

IM-er: Andrea . . . you're teasing me
IM-er: lol
Girl: and how to say butterfly in Hebrew from one of my friends
Girl: nope
Girl: muchos besos?
Girl: lol
Girl: sorry
IM-er: lol
Girl: ps. I've had artwork shown in a gallery
Girl: art history undergrad . . . switched careers bc apparently I can't save the world w marketing campaigns.
IM-er: :)
Girl: I tried but felt unfulfilled
Girl: activity level is seleted activities?
Girl: what does that even mean?lol

     Here, I had to try to contain myself. As you can probably imagine, I was getting very annoyed. I had already made it crystal clear that I wanted her number, but she continued to change the subject on me. And, more annoyingly, she continues to talk about herself when she wasn't asked. It's becoming obnoxious.

IM-er: let me explain mouth to ear
Girl: ok

```
IM-er:  great
IM-er:  so, let's exchange numbers
Girl:   I gg gym in a few . . .
IM-er:  ###-####
IM-er:  I'll call you around 9:45?
Girl:   e-mail me first . . . .I'll be there till 11. have 6 miles to
        jog
Girl:   ?
```

In some cases, especially when a conversation is extremely short, an e-mail address can be an acceptable compromise, but certainly *not* after a conversation this long and intense. At this point, it would be insulting for her to expect me to settle for an e-mail address because it probably won't lead to a date.

Remember, you aren't looking for a pen pal, and if need be, say that. You are looking to find a companion. You are trying to make a connection with someone. Intermittent e-mail exchanges often lead nowhere, because it limits the communication, which can create a greater challenge in establishing energy. The more you limit your communication, the less personal it becomes.

```
IM-er:  Lol. I'm not looking for a pen-pal.
IM-er:  how about a text?
```

At this point, if you're going to continue pursuing this girl, you need her number or you will be wasting your time.

```
Girl:   lol
IM-er:  It's more personal
Girl:   convince me?
```

"Convince me"? That made me think, *Ugh. Really? You need me to stroke your ego a bit more?* What further convincing does she want? She claims to have enjoyed our dialog for the past half hour.

IM-er: Andrea, you've been enjoying our conversation for about a half hour. You should already be convinced.

Don't ever hesitate to show confidence within the context of IM. If you establish a strong balance, it is reasonable for you to expect to exchange phone numbers.

Girl: ?

Now that you've established subject balance, you are both on the same page regarding the topic of discussion, so you can pull back on your aggressiveness. She isn't ignoring your request anymore. I recommend you try to be cute in this circumstance, if, of course, that's natural for you. Remain calm.

Now, she is challenging me and has told me what I need to do to get her phone number. I can either do it and succeed (Option A) or, refuse, call her bluff and likely walk away without her phone number, saving dignity, but certainly not the productive route. (Option B). As you can see, I went with Option A.

IM-er: I think the puppy deserves a treat
IM-er: lol
Girl: ?
Girl: now you r a puppu?
Girl: puppy?
IM-er: I thought it was cute

Girl: lay it on thick and you got the digits
Girl: a good one
Girl: I know you have it in you
Girl: lol

So, now she's outright told me to "lay it on thick."
I had come this far, so wasn't going to let dignity or
pride hold me back.

In a situation like this, *if you want it*, you have to
go the extra mile to get it.

IM-er: haha
IM-er: hmmm
Girl: take your time
IM-er: I've never been this stimulated from an IM conversation
         in my life..
IM-er: literally . . .

The truth is, when you get involved in a long IM
conversation with someone you're first getting to
know, challenging and witty banter may be annoying
to deal with at moments but will often keep you interested. You may be wondering, *Why does he bother
putting up with this crap?* Well, for two reasons.
One, we're all ultimately looking for someone who
can keep us interested and hold up their end of the
conversation. Two, you must remember that wom-
en often will naturally be more guarded within the
context of an initial IM conversation to ward off men
who aren't looking for a relationship. As a result, we
can expect them to be extra challenging in the initial
stages of online dating conversations. Their purpose
is to avoid those who are looking only to hook up.

Girl: awwwww

Girl: ok. almost there
Girl: ha

If she becomes what I call a "brat," call her out on it. Don't let her treat you like a circus attraction. It's okay that she's demanding effort, but you should demand she be reasonable. If you let her get away with what she wants online, she will assume she can do that offline too.

IM-er: haha
IM-er: you've gotta be kidding with me
Girl: a little
IM-er: I've given you an army
Girl: but if you say the right thing I've never heard . . . it'd be a nice surprise
IM-er: can't give away the whole arsenal without the proper coordinates
Girl: an army?
IM-er: lol
Girl: ok.
Girl: I feel let down
Girl: :(
IM-er: wait
IM-er: ok
IM-er: ok
Girl: I'm trying to challenge you
Girl: to open up
Girl: I'm not a cold person
IM-er: If you're seriously this beautiful, communicative, and full of energy. I'm just happy we were able to connect

I did think her pictures were beautiful and believed she was communicative. At times she was sweet and verbally affectionate, but, let's be honest. She's been really feisty, at moments obnoxious, and has gone well out of her way to challenge me at every possible turn. She's been a major pain, but since I put in so much time, it's only logical to finish what I've started and give her the benefit of my doubt. After all, if I were interested enough to entertain the conversation for this long, it's worth the extra effort to see if she was just being overly guarded to ward off online players (OLPs).

I'd just like to elaborate on what really makes this conversation with Andrea such a pain: her communicative intensity. Really. There is no better word than "intense" to describe her communication style. She was literally all over the place throughout most of our IM conversation. It's exhausting to communicate with someone who continuously moves from one subject to another, and it can be difficult to keep up with frequent non-sequiturs. She rarely gave me a chance to answer a question before asking another. This could be well described as IM diarrhea—she may as well have been communicating with herself. But, in all fairness, because I've written a whole book, I'm sure I have been guilty at times.

Girl:	awww
Girl:	ok
Girl:	you used my own words against me but it works
Girl:	I'd say that to you
IM-er:	what words?
Girl:	###-####
Girl:	I am grateful you are just yourself
Girl:	thank you for being you
IM-er:	you are really sweet, Andrea

Unfortunately, she has already given me her number,

so if she throws an "I am grateful you are just yourself" at me, I have to reciprocate; otherwise, she would feel self-conscious about putting herself out there.

However, "you are really sweet, Andrea," was the most I was willing to give at this point because she has demanded so much throughout the conversation.

Girl: awwwww
Girl: sealed
Girl: call sometime def
Girl: I gg . . . workout time :)

Now, I'm good to go. For the record, I'm relieved this conversation is over. I just relived this experience by breaking it down for you, and it was awkward, like watching the movie, *Meet the Parents*, and feeling for the protagonist.

IM-er: tonight, or tomorrow?
Girl: surprise me silly
IM-er: haha, will do
Girl: whenever you feel like you want to
Girl: I'm at the gym until 11
Girl: steamroom
IM-er: phew . . . I'll text you tonight . . . you can let me know when you're back :)
IM-er: sound good?
Girl: k
Girl: your sweet
Girl: ttyl

<<<<<<< IM Conversation Ended >>>>>>>

Looking back, this is such a frustrating conversation to read. Why did I entertain the conversation for so long? I was being somewhat shallow, but I was also trying to give Andrea the benefit of my doubt. Eventually, even if I decided not to pursue a follow-up date before ending the conversation, I would have felt I had put in too much time to end the conversation without getting her phone number and giving her a chance. Yes, she became increasingly more annoying and challenging throughout the conversation; however, I was taught not to judge a book only by its cover, which in this case is not just someone's pictures, but annoyance associated with her nervousness. The cover is the first impression, remember.

Unfortunately, Andrea was just as annoying when we met in person as she was when we communicated online. Learn from my mistakes . . . don't just put up with extreme frustration to get a cute date. If you don't think you will be able to move past the initial frustration from an online chat, it will not be a good use of your time to pursue the follow-up date. It will likely leave you with a bad taste in your mouth, metaphorically speaking . . . it's often difficult to change our minds after a negative first impression.

So, what is the most effective way to exit a frustrating online conversation? There are many ways you can do so, two of which are:

1. Simply say, "I have to get going. Have a good ___" (fill in the blank)

2. Be boring, quiet or non-chatty to eliminate her interest in you—she will likely not want to continue chatting

Option "1" is fast and easy, and while it's not a nice way to end a conversation (because you won't be offering someone a chance to say "goodbye" or to get back in touch at a later time), it's not mean either. Either way, both options are the least of evils because they don't require you to directly tell someone you're not interested.

Chapter 6

Conversations with Emilie and Gina:
Developing Rapport Quickly

What is the point of a *jump start*? If you don't have much time to talk, but don't want to wait to connect with someone until later, a jump start can be an effective strategy. This tactic can also be helpful to a person who is concerned about not being successful via IM. Certainly, I am confident in my IM skills; however, there were times when I was simply too tired or didn't have enough time to have a long conversation. A jump start was a great way to avoid procrastinating communication and facilitate a potential connection.

Since a jump start likely yields a shorter conversation, this chapter will feature two short IM exchanges that serve as examples of jump starts.

Emilie

IM-er: hey there, Emilie

<<<<<<< Waiting to Connect >>>>>>>

You will note that I refer to Emilie by her first name before ever connecting with her. Just so you know I'm not psychic, Emilie had used her first name as her username.

IM-er: wow, you're stunning

A great way to initiate a jump start is to begin with an enthusiastic, powerful greeting. I recommend this to achieve rapid success by generating energy quickly. The rationale behind this concept is a quick "in and out" execution. You're determined to be so quick that you minimize your chance to screw up, which is easiest when you make a powerful first impression with an enthusiastic compliment, right off the bat. To achieve a jump start, you must be prepared to make your move within one minute of when she first responds.

<<<<<<< Waiting to Connect >>>>>>>

IM-er: so glad we have the chance to connect :)

<<<<<<< Waiting to Connect >>>>>>>

<<<<<<< Connected >>>>>>>

Girl: thank you.. How was your day?

IM-er: good . . . definitely good
IM-er: but
IM-er: I'm tired . . .
IM-er: gotta head to sleep soon
IM-er: but
IM-er: been hoping to get to know you
IM-er: I'd really like to continue our convo . . . .
IM-er: let's exchange numbers, and I'll throw you a text
        tomorrow

Genuine, logical, yet respectfully aggressive.

Girl: hmm id rather talk on the phone than text tommorow...
        what do you think?
Girl: its more personal

This is an ideal scenario.

IM-er: lol . . . sure
IM-er: absolutely

Enthusiasm can be contagious.

IM-er: my number is ###-###-####
IM-er: what's yours?
Girl: mine is ###-###-####.
Girl: awesome:)
IM-er: I'm very much looking forward to talking to you
IM-er: Emilie, can I text you in the morning, to say hi?
IM-er: that cool?

Usually, I wouldn't recommend consecutively repeated questions, especially this early in a conversation, but a jump start is predicated on a conversation with time constraints.

Girl: haha yea sure..as long as you like to also talk via voice
        lol
IM-er: of course
IM-er: I am a singer/songwriter; never the shy type. I definitely
        don't mind talking on the phone.
IM-er: ok . . . I will definitely text and call you tomorrow

> You don't want to end the conversation without
> establishing minimal balance. If you fail to establish
> minimal balance, you most likely will never connect
> with her again.

Girl: oh ooh i sing too!!
Girl: we could do a duet
IM-er: sweeeet

> In a quick conversation, specifically a jump start,
> you have to be enthusiastic 100% of the time—short,
> sweet and effective.

Girl: i looove it
IM-er: me too!
IM-er: and.. you're beautiful
Girl: so i guess u like that combination?
IM-er: hellz yea
IM-er: lol
IM-er: sweet, sensitive, affectionate. +

> "Sweet," "sensitive" and "affectionate," were all
> words used in Emilie's profile to describe herself.

IM-er: oh yes
IM-er: A great combination . . . to me :)

> This is what I refer to as a *combo re-enforcer*.

While I already got her number and established minimal balance, my goal is to trigger her excitement. A combo re-enforcer lets her know why you're intrigued, which consists of different personal attributes, followed by "a great combination" (or substitute your adjective) to enforce genuine enthusiasm. This triggers excitement.

Girl: yes and do you think u are also those things?
IM-er: 100%
IM-er: excited?
IM-er: ;)

Once you've been given her number, don't be afraid to ask if she's excited. She'll probably say yes, and if she does it will likely trigger a positive mental association with you. The goal of a jump start is to create immediate excitement, and to be remembered by this excitement for the follow-up call.

Girl: i am excited..being excited about different
          conversations and meetings in life is key in my mind
IM-er: I can appreciate that. Ok, well . . . Sweet dreams,
          Emilie

When saying good night, if it has been a success, don't say "Good night," say "Sweet dreams." It's sweet, cute, personal, and sounds more confident and flirtatious than "good night."

IM-er: Looking forward to talking to you tomorrow
Girl: sleep well;)
IM-er: I will, and I'll text you in the morning
IM-er: ;)
Girl: sounds good..now u have to go to sleep lol

IM-er: yep. Sweet dreams, Emilie :)

It's never a good idea to repeat something more than once, unless you have to, especially "Sweet dreams." It will lose its effectiveness if it's said more than two times because it will seem like you say it to every girl, every time, all the time. It's important that you try to make every girl you speak to feel important, and, of course, it should be genuine. People like to feel special, so give them a reason to.

IM-er: tty in the morning

<<<<<<< IM Conversation Ended >>>>>>>

A jump start is based on developing the majority of your initial rapport via phone, and since the IM communication is so limited, I am providing a second example: Gina.

Gina

IM-er: hey there

<<<<<<< Waiting to Connect >>>>>>>

IM-er: I'm Keith

<<<<<<< Waiting to Connect >>>>>>>

<<<<<<< Connected >>>>>>>

Girl: hi—i'm Gina
Girl: how are ya?
IM-er: Hi Gina
IM-er: I'm good
IM-er: gettin ready to go to lunch soon . . . wow, you're the
         first Jewish girl I've spoken to named Gina

I knew she was Jewish based on the information
she included in her profile.

IM-er: such a beautiful name
Girl: why thank you
IM-er: and.. since I already started with the compliments . . .
Girl: how sweet

Balance is now established.

IM-er: such a beautiful smile

To initiate a jump start, I'm repeating beautiful
to use consistent, complimentary wording to help
make a powerful first impression.

Girl: well keep them coming . . . .i'm definitely a girly girl so
         compliments are my favs :)
IM-er: well
IM-er: it's nice when the girl I'm going for has things to
         compliment
Girl: awwww so how come you're going for a girl 3 years
         older than you? hope that doesn't sound defensive . . .
         just curious
IM-er: I was hoping you would respond to my IM . . .
IM-er: just for that reason, I thought you might not
IM-er: honestly . . . I have two reasons
IM-er: first of all... I generally don't

IM-er: nothing against it, but, generally girls 3 years older than me only like dating older men
IM-er: but,
Girl: yezzzz
IM-er: my two reasons are.. 1. I think you're beautiful and 2. I'm looking for something more serious

As you can see from Gina's interruption with "yezzzz," it's a powerful technique to pause when providing an explanation to an important question. Not surprisingly, I call these *explanation pauses*. By pausing, you trigger a build-up of anticipation, which creates excitement. If you provide an answer she likes, she will respond with more excitement, which helps generate a positive balance shift.

Girl: good answers :)
Girl: well i have to get back to work but text me sometime . . . would be fun to meetup in person. ###-###-####
IM-er: that would be great
IM-er: mine is ###-###-####

<<<<<<< IM Conversation Ended >>>>>>>

The goal of this book is to teach you what I haven't seen taught anywhere else: real-time dialog strategies, focusing on the context of IM conversation. With that in mind, I understand that different people are comfortable in different circumstances. Some people are more comfortable on the phone than others; for those who would prefer to limit IM communication, a jump start might work for you.

Chapter 7

Conversation:
Communicating Effectively with E-mail

The strategies I have taught you are applicable throughout the pre-dating and in-person dating processes. Obviously, when you meet in person, you will not use a keyboard to communicate; but, remember, effective communication is effective communication, regardless of the setting. While this book focuses mainly on the intricacies of IM communication, I certainly will never discount the usefulness of e-mail; it's how I connected with my wife, Stephanie.

Your E-mail Strategy

The strategy used for instant messaging will work for e-mailing; however, e-mail strategy should be based on two main factors: writing skills and efficiency.

Writing skills

Whereas instant message takes place in real time, e-mail gives you the opportunity to perfect your message; you have no excuse to make grammatical or punctuation errors. You certainly don't want to come across as too formal, because that's just weird and off-putting. Just like when instant messaging, you should always introduce yourself, which is proper. When I say, "Don't be too formal," I mean not to come across as being stiff. For instance, your e-mail to an online dater should not read the way your college application essay would or did. You should present yourself in an organized and intelligent fashion. Remember: An e-mail will likely be read with more attentive eyes than an instant message conversation because an e-mail is likely written and read within a less time-sensitive setting.

In all fairness, a little mistake here or there won't hurt you, but if you send a carelessly written e-mail with poor grammar, without punctuation and/or lacking energy, you're going to come across as illiterate, stupid and most likely unappealing. Again, within an e-mail, you have no excuse to send a message like that because you have as much time as you need to edit and perfect your message. Here are some basic grammar rules for e-mailing:

- When your sentences end, there should always be a period (.)
- Each of your questions should end with a question mark (?)
- An occasional comma (,) wouldn't hurt your cause.
- Paragraphs should be used to separate your thoughts, which makes you seem organized. You create each new paragraph by pressing *enter* or *return*. Paragraphing also makes your e-mail easier on the eyes and on the brain.

Efficiency

While mastering instant message gives you the opportunity to generate much initial energy, an e-mail can be a
powerful means of communication as well. If someone is
interested enough in you to open and read your first e-mail
communication, they will judge you on a number of factors,
some of which you have more control over than others:

- Profile pictures
- Substance/quality of your e-mail
- Profile write-up

To maximize your chances of getting responses to e-
mail, you want to "incentivize" the recipient. I use "incentivize" to remind you of what I mentioned in the beginning of this
book: Online dating success is directly linked to your ability to
sell yourself, so you should highlight your best features.

When someone receives your e-mail, their decision to
respond is going to be based on your pictures, e-mail quality
and profile write-up. If someone finds your pictures semi-
attractive, then your writing a great, thoughtful e-mail might
push that person over the edge and give you a better chance
of getting a response. While there is always someone more
attractive, your goal should be to present yourself as the
most intriguing. Remember, beauty will eventually fade, but
you can always make your personality shine.

Develop a Template

An e-mail template is an e-mail you formulate in your
word processor or within an e-mail to yourself. It should be
intended to intrigue daters who posses the attributes you
seek in a potential match. Examples of such attributes may
include, but are not limited to:

- Sweet
- Outgoing
- Sensitive
- Nurturing

Ideally, you will find that a number of your matches describe themselves as having (many of) the same attributes as one another within their profiles. This is ideal because it demonstrates consistency in the matches you are seeking. Your goal is to pinpoint these common features and develop a creative way to express genuine appreciation for the attributes you admire.

It may be helpful to create a cheat sheet. This is a good way to brainstorm ideas. You can use your cheat sheet to come up with:

Openers *(example):*

- "Hey there,
  just came across your profile and I'm really intrigued :) "

Recognition of Attributes *(example):*

- "First of all, your pictures are adorable. That's a great place to start . . . and, when reading on, you describe yourself with so many attributes I'm looking for: sweet, outgoing, sensitive . . ." (You do not have to actually use the word "attribute" when recognizing an attribute.)

Closes *(example):*

- "I hope to hear back from you and have the opportunity to get to know you."

In putting together your e-mail template, copy elements and comments from your cheat sheet and paste into your template those that are applicable to your intended match.

Your template should not read like a form letter; rather, it should be personalized for the type of person you're looking for. Once you've developed an e-mail template that yields a good response rate, you can copy and paste different elements that apply to different online daters who capture your interest. There is nothing wrong with recycling a successful e-mail template; in fact, it's fine strategy.

You must remember that an e-mail template should only be used when appropriate. Once your initial e-mail gets a reply, your responses thereafter should be customized—you should not use an e-mail template as a response to an e-mail. If an e-mail gets a reply, it gives you another opportunity to shine, so you should put together the best response you can think of and then perfect it.

The following is based on the e-mail chain that led to the relationship with my wife. I have broken down the key elements of the dialog the same way I have throughout the book so you can understand why I wrote what I wrote, how I interpret everything, and how and why I responded the way I did.

After stumbling upon Stephanie's profile, I was determined to connect with her. She was a beautiful girl with a beautiful smile. Better yet, I felt she was intelligent and seemed to share many of the same interests as me. Simply put, when reading Stephanie's profile, I immediately had the sense that we would click. I was never able to instant message her because I didn't ever see Stephanie online when I was logged into my account, so I chose to e-mail her because I was eager to initiate communication . . . I'm grateful that I did.

E-mail to Stephanie from Keith

Hey there,

I'm Keith.

Even though I've explained it many times through-out the book, repetition facilitates the learning pro-cess: A proper introduction is crucial and should be habitual, such as my saying, "Hey. I'm Keith." That hardly requires any effort but yields a far greater first impression than "Yo waz up hotness."

First of all, I must call a spade "a spade" when I see it—you are gorgeous. You know where pretty meets beautiful?—Well, you take it to another level :) Corny, but true. And, while I'm sure you get nice compliments all the time, I figured it would be a nice way to put an original spin on it. So, that's definitely the first thing I noticed.

When using an e-mail template, it's important to create something original. Always try to avoid writing the same things other online daters write, especially when complimenting someone. Since it is virtually impossible to know what other online daters write within their private messages, other than what a fel-low friend online dater may share with you, your best bet is to put forth effort. Try to write something you don't feel sounds generic. Above, I write: "you are gorgeous." While "gorgeous" is a common word, it's less overused than "hot"; however, what's most origi-nal here is the use of "I must call a spade a spade," which I use to precede the compliment. I've found that preceding a compliment, opinion or statement with different phrases and/or introductions helps maximize the delivery. Every e-mail presents an opportunity to sell, present and perform; the way in which something is sold, presented and performed is its *delivery*, which is what makes it authentic.

Authenticating your words can be done in a variety of ways, but it all comes down to delivery and follow-through. Above, you will note that after I tell Stephanie she's gorgeous, I follow it up with a creative explanation: "you know where pretty meets beautiful?—Well, you take it to another level." In this circumstance, while I am being sweet, I am also very overly sentimental—to make an effort that few others are willing to make—which is why I take a stab at myself by saying, "Corny, but true." By doing that, you disable the reader from passing negative judgment on you by making fun of yourself and taking pride in your words. It shows confidence when you can laugh at yourself, and you have more control when you take the lead.

I've also found that ending each paragraph with a positive thought helps create a warm vibe for the reader. Remember, your goal is to elicit a response by incentivizing the recipient. The best approach is to be optimistic and intriguing. If you're not, why would someone want to respond?

I'm glad to see that we both share such a strong passion for music—as far as I'm concerned, it's a crucial thing to look for in finding someone, just because of how important it is in my life.

Note how I created a small paragraph—even though it doesn't technically qualify as a paragraph.

This allows the reader's eyes to rest for a moment and gives the writer an opportunity to organize thoughts.

It's beneficial to share positive points with the reader, such as having the same interests or passions. In this e-mail exchange, I draw attention to the fact that we're both passionate about music.

I love the fact that you're a first grade teacher—I get the sense that you probably are really sweet and have lots of patience.

Again, I create a paragraph to begin a new thought—this time to express my appreciation for Stephanie's career.

Remember, when you give a compliment that's intended to show genuine interest—not focusing on someone's looks—the best delivery is to rationalize your compliment: "I get the sense that you are probably really sweet and have lots of patience."

Seeing that we're a "match," I have to imagine that we'd have a lot in common—either way, I'm sure the conversation wouldn't be dull.

Yes, another paragraph. The reason why this looks good to the reader is because it shows you took the time to organize your thoughts and gives the e-mail a greater sense of authenticity.

In that brief paragraph, I utilized an online dating site's match-percentage indicator, a computer-generated percentage based on common answers to generic questions—to reinforce the possibility of Stephanie and I being a great match. But, realistically, this match percentage is based on an algorithm, for which the results may not hold any real dating chemistry-based value other than your willingness to recognize it. It's an interesting talking point or ice-breaker, but it's not the "be all end all," so I follow up my comment with "either way, I'm sure the conversation wouldn't be dull."

Definitely hoping to hear back from you.

-Keith

Note how I sign off by writing: "-Keith." It is not necessarily the right way to sign off, and it's not crucial for you to sign off at all; however, I always do. A sign off is representative of a more formal writing style and is just my personal preference. As you know from the preceding chapters, I am a strong advocate of consistency, which is why I always sign off.

Avoid feeling too confident that you'll get a reply from a first e-mail. It's important to show interest, but it can be really off putting if you seem cocky. "Hoping to hear back from you" is a great way to accomplish both.

E-Mail from Stephanie to Keith

Hi Keith.

It's always good when someone replies to your first e-mail that they address you by your first name; it shows engagement. This is not to say that it's bad when the reply is "hey," without addressing you by your name, but I always prefer for someone to address me by my name.

That was a really nice message you sent me. Usually, when someone makes a comment about how I look, I immediately disregard them, but yours was sweet, not creepy and pervy. So, thank you. You made me smile today.

Always read carefully what someone writes. In this e-mail, Stephanie writes: "usually when someone makes a comment about how I look, I immediately disregard them." So, for future reference, I will be sparing with aesthetic compliments.

Also note that Stephanie writes "but yours was sweet," and then writes "you made me smile to-day." The keys are being "sweet" and "you made me smile," so my goal is to continue being sweet and to repeat her words: "you made me smile." I like to repeat things like this in an e-mail chain; it reinforces the positive energy from the e-mail.

So, where are you from?

Obviously, this isn't a deep question, but it's good because it shows that Stephanie is making an effort to continue the e-mail dialog.

Stephanie does not sign off at the end of her e-mail to me. There is nothing wrong with that; it is her personal preference, which is representative of a more casual style.

E-Mail from Keith to Stephanie

Hey there, Stephanie

Just as I like to be addressed by my first name, so do others; it shows respect and engagement.

I'm so glad that I was able to make you smile—getting a response from you actually had that effect on me. In case you couldn't tell, I did put time into that e-mail because I'm really interested in connecting with you; your profile resonated with me.

Remember how I told you to reinforce positive energy from previous e-mails? The example above is a good way to accomplish that: "I'm so glad that I was able to make you smile." You can build upon generated energy by reciprocating the energy: "you actually had that effect on me."

As you can see, I took it a step farther by telling Stephanie why I put time into my e-mail. Note how I wrote: "your profile resonated with me." When using less-common words and expressions, your e-mail becomes more genuine and therefore seems more authentic.

Why did it make me smile? Well, (aside from the above reasoning) this has been a very tough week for me... I've been working out really hard at the gym. I was up to 4 miles per/day + a weight workout. So, Saturday night, after my run and workout, I was headed to the supermarket to get groceries to make myself dinner before meeting up with my friends - on my way to the supermarket, I slipped on ice and broke the two main bones in my right ankle, so I'm in a cast and crutches for probably 3 months(ish). I'm going to be somewhat limited these days (even though I manage to get myself to the gym everyday). So, point being, I was really hoping to hear back from you because when I read your profile, I made up my mind that I'm very interested. So, getting a response made me really happy.

Please note that this paragraph is situational; however, I chose to use this e-mail exchange for two reasons: 1) This e-mail exchange led to my getting married, and 2) I had broken my ankle before meeting Stephanie, which is to show you that personality is the main determinant in a successful e-mail dialog. (You will note that even after Stephanie finds out I am on crutches, she continues to show interest.)

Again, I find an opportunity to reinforce positive energy: "why did it make me smile?" I then follow my explanation up with: "I was really hoping to hear back from you because . . . I'm very interested." The reason I did that was to build upon the positive energy; hence, "So, getting a response made me really happy."

After reading the same BS over and over from profile to profile, yours is a breath of fresh air :) I truly mean that.

Try to not overuse emoticons; they quickly lose their novelty and become ineffective. The above :) is only the second time I used one in the e-mail dialog. When using an emoticon, make sure it is placement appropriate, such as after a compliment.

I think it's both cute and cool that you were in band

when you were younger—what instrument?

Personalize, personalize and personalize more. The more personalized your e-mail is, the more engaged you seem; the more engaged you seem, the more engaged the reader becomes.

Note how I comment on Stephanie's participating in band when she was younger, better yet, I show interest by asking about the instrument she played.

I'm not necessarily a fan of all your favorite bands, but most certainly respect your taste, as anyone that loves Radiohead must know their shit—they epitomize creative musicianship.

You don't necessarily have to agree with every opinion or share every interest someone has, but it's always good to show interest in knowing their interests. Even if you don't share an interest, you can respect any differences.

I live on the UES, are you in Manhattan often?

I'm going to be moving out to Queens in June (the end of my lease). I love Queens—it's tough to be leaving Manhattan, but where else can I find a huge 1-bedroom for the price I pay for a studio in Manhattan? Lol.

I look forward to hearing back from you.

-Keith

In the first e-mail, I suggest closing with something such as, "I hope to hear back from you," because you want to show genuine interest;

but initially you should avoid coming across as too sure of yourself. That isn't to say that you shouldn't be confident, but you can't *assume* the recipient will reply, you should only hope.

After you've received a reply from an online dater, it is safe to end following e-mails with "I look forward to hearing back from you," because at this point, they've already shown interest in you.

E-Mail from Stephanie to Keith

What's your number? I think texting would be easier.

You may notice, in Stephanie's response, she does not address me by my name this time. Well, it obviously doesn't bother me because she's asking for my number. Generally, I prefer to be given a phone number versus being asked for mine, but in this circumstance, I hadn't mentioned phone numbers yet, so it shows Stephanie is taking the initiative, which is great.

I actually live in Queens—my lease is up in May and my roommate is moving to Brooklyn. I'm not sure where I'll be in a few months lol. If I still know you, I'll let you know.

Stephanie writes above, "If I still know you . . ." Don't let something like this faze you. Obviously, since we have not met or even spoken on the phone, Stephanie is going to be at least somewhat skeptical that things will work out, so she makes a playful comment. Remember, she has made the effort to write me back and just asked for my phone number so, it shouldn't bother you (at all) that someone makes a comment like that. In all fairness, it's completely logical for her to make that comment.

I can't believe you broke your ankle. That sucks. I happen to be a klutz, so accidents happen to me all the time. When I go away on vacation with my friend Rachel, the first place she looks for is the infirmary.

This e-mail from Stephanie is a response to the e-mail explaining my injury, and she's still interested even though I'm injured and in a cast with crutches. That shows how all your petty insecurities are only as problematic is you allow them to be; in other words, if you don't see it as a problem, mostly likely no one else will either. So, be confident and be proud of who you are and what you are.

Stephanie writes: "I can't believe . . ." followed by, "That sucks," followed by "I happen to be." This demonstrated Stephanie is not turned off by the fact that I'm injured; in fact, she shows empathy and tries to relate.

Three years ago in the Bahamas, I stepped on a bee and had a Shrek foot and lots of cute wedges I could not wear.

E-Mail from Keith to Stephanie

Haha—cool. So, I'm not the only one.

Yea, sure—texting would most definitely be easier. My number is ###-####.

For the record, when I move to Queens, I will have a car, so I'm not too concerned :p

As I mentioned above about Stephanie's "If I still know you" comment, it's a completely logical thing to think or say. There's no need for me to make a reference to the comment; however, it's just my style.

What's your number?

There are two ways to go about this last e-mail; as you can see, I chose to provide my number, as well as ask Stephanie for hers. Just so you aren't concerned, should this circumstance present itself, there is no correct way to proceed. Your options are:

1. Give your number and anticipate a text/phone call but not ask for their phone number
2. Give your number and ask for their phone number

I'm looking forward to hearing back from you :)

-Keith

At this point, it's okay to throw in an extra emoticon—if it represents your personality. If you've been asked to give out your number or have been given someone's number, it's normal to be excited and enthusiastic; it won't hurt to express it.

All in all, you will note that the same strategy used in IM can be applied to e-mail. As shown in the example above, the main difference is instant message requires quick-witted strategy and does not provide much of a window for you to correct spelling, grammar and punctuation.

To maintain IM energy, you need to be able to communicate quickly, hence "instant." In an e-mail, you need to structure your message in an organized fashion and utilize the time that you have to perfect the content before sending.

The most important advice I can give you regarding e-mail is to take your time.

Chapter 8

Conversation:
Directing Dialog

Directing dialog is essentially steering the conversation flow to maintain balance between you and your potential match. There are varying levels of conversational balance, which can be categorized by three distinct stages: minimal, solid and strong.

Minimal balance is established when your match responds to your initial communication attempt and demonstrates the willingness to engage in conversation by expanding on a topic or asking some questions. This stage is ideally reached quickly, likely within the first 2–5 minutes (unless someone allows the conversation to be interrupted by something such as a phone call).

Solid balance is best described by rapport that reflects engagement from both you and your match; however, at this stage, you have not yet reached a level of mutual enthusiasm to meet in person. Solid balance is usually reached within the first 5–15 minutes. At this point, you have made a connection, but it still needs to be developed. To accomplish this, find things in common, reveal vulnerabilities and establish yourself as being genuine and unique. A strong balance is reached when you and your match establish rapport consisting of reciprocal, active engagement. Developing strong balance requires time, energy and mutual enthusiasm; it could take at least 25–40 minutes to develop this level of rapport. At this stage, you and your match will feel generally comfortable with one another's personalities and, most importantly, both express the desire to continue getting to know each other.

Once you've made a connection, she will exert effort. For example, if you were to stop typing for an extended period, she would feel compelled to IM you. In most circumstances, establishing a strong balance will require you to direct the dialog, most effectively accomplished with questions and topic transitions.

Questioning

Questioning is your opportunity to get to know someone you've identified as a potential match. Find out everything you can. Beyond the information you read within a dater's profile, you will know only what the person tells you. Before your first IM, read her profile carefully to develop questions you might ask. If she didn't fill out her profile thoughtfully, expect that she's likely not an active online dater and, therefore, may be less likely to respond. If she didn't bother to fill out her profile, unless you're highly experienced, it's extremely difficult to ask strategic questions.

After sending your initial message and receiving a response, be ready with an articulate compliment, such as, "You really are adorable." You want to make it evident that you're excited to *connect* with her. If your compliment seems genuine to her, she will feel special. She should sense your excitement.

Make sure everything you ask has a purpose, which can be merely to stimulate conversation. Your goal is to avoid getting stuck with nothing to say. When you get an answer to a question, you always want to quickly transition to the next subject or to your follow-up response.

If you can think of a unique way to ask a question, or ask a question that's unique, it will make you seem more interesting. Sometimes, however, questions should just be asked in a straightforward manner. If you can't think of a creative way to ask an important question, you should still ask. It shouldn't feel like work.

Before you meet in person, doesn't it make sense to determine if you're compatible? Consider the following questions and topics of conversation:

Where did she grow up?

"So, where'd you grow up . . . was it one of those small towns with privately owned supermarkets?" or "Was it easy to have fun?"

(Ask the question in a way that shows you are interested in her answer.)

What does she do for work?

"So, how do you keep yourself busy all day?"

(Ask if she enjoys it. Is it just a job or her career?)

What does she do for fun?

"So, what's your favorite thing to do on a Friday night? Is it any different on a Saturday night?" or, "Do you find Friday night's vibe different than Saturday nights?"

(Make note of what is she doing in her pictures and ask about it.)

"Wow . . . did you run the marathon?"

What is she wearing in her pictures?

"You look adorable in your first pic. Are you more of a tank-top and sweat pants type of girl?"

What TV shows and movies does she watch?

"Would you rather watch American Idol or Mad Men?"

Does she have a pet?

"Are you more of a dog person or cat person?"

Does she have allergies?

(It can help you go on a trouble-free first date to know to avoid certain foods or certain locations.)

Where did she go to school?

"How many colleges did you visit?" or "Dare I ask . . . did you have the 'Animal House' experience?"

(You can spark a side conversation. Use the answer as insight. For example, if she visited many schools while searching for college, it may be indicative that she likely takes her time before making a decision—or choosing a mate.)

What did/does she study?

Was/is she an English major? If so, will presenting a good vocabulary and grammar skills give you an edge?

More Questions and Elements to Consider

- How does she relate to others, and who is in her life?
- Does she have siblings? Were there any other people in her pictures?
- How many pictures does she have in her profile?
- Does she pose? In a classy or provocative manner?
- Does she reveal any personality traits through her pictures? Does her smile seem bubbly? Or does it seem warm?
- Is she hugging people with genuine enthusiasm in her pictures?
- Does she seem affectionate?
- Does she speak other languages?
- Does she travel?
- Has she traveled? If yes, where? If no, does she want to?
- Is she artistic?
- Does she dance?
- Does she draw/paint/sculpt? If no, did she ever? Is this something you both have in common?
- Is she musical? What's her favorite genre of music? Do you both like similar music?
- Does she like going to any particular parks?
Does she ever go to museums?

Review of Overall Concepts

Re-read my previous conversations in Chapters 1–5. Note how I phrased my questions and how I transition from topic to topic. If you direct dialog and establish a strong balance by asking important and unique questions, you will get useful answers and provoke enthusiasm. If you get enthusiastic responses, you will get more details. Details help create context. Context can also be created through discussing thought-provoking topics, which helps you become acquainted with one another. When she opts to give you details, you've provoked her to think. The more details you obtain, the more context you can create. Once there is context, there's a foundation for strong balance. She's exerting energy in the conversation if she begins to ask you questions; in this case, you can direct the dialog.

Balance

Once you have mastered the skill of creating and maintaining balance, it's all about IM-ing and context. As soon as she responds to your IM, you need to reply to her in real time. But it's crucial when you ask a question that you give her two to three minutes to answer you. If she is flaky within the first 30 seconds, other than her phone ringing just as you connect, it is likely she's probably not going to give you a chance. Remember, the moment she IMs you, she's at her computer, but at any moment she could get up and walk away. If that happens, any generated energy can be lost.

There is only one strategy you can use to try to avoid losing energy: The moment she IMs you, get involved and try to intrigue her as quickly as you can until you've established solid balance. You need to allow, at the very least, a few minutes to establish solid balance. She will then be less inclined to allow an interruption in the conversation.

Transitioning

Once you've established a solid balance, shifting toward a strong balance requires you to dig for details by asking multiple important questions, but remember to do so in a unique way. After you're given details, you can give occasional backhanded compliments, which will shift the energy. Backhanded compliments help shift energy because they are more likely to elicit a response, such as, "What do you mean?" which gives you control over the direction of dialog. (Please refer to the earlier explanation of negs.) If you give a straightforward compliment, such as "You're beautiful," you've told her only what she wants to hear, but that won't necessarily prompt her to respond with anything other than "Thanks."

Remember, your goal is to intrigue and compel her to exert energy. If you both exert energy, you're at social balance, but if you can influence the level of energy she exerts, you direct the flow of dialog. For example, if she's telling you about a wedding she went to and how she cried during the ceremony, you can comment on her sensitivity, such as when I said, "I'd imagine that it's a fair assumption that you tear during chick flicks." That seems like a question, but it's more of a statement that will likely tempt her to respond.

"Assumption" is a key word. Don't say something mean, but by "assuming" something about her personality, she will likely be inclined to respond, agree or defend herself, even if she's not being insulted. If she responds with energy, you've established a stronger balance. If your assumption is right, great! If your assumption is wrong, but she defends herself, remember that she cares enough to explain herself. Energy is good.

When she answers your IM, I advise that your responses be genuine, complimentary and quick. An effective way to establish energy quickly is to ask questions faster than she asks you. Remember, people generally love when others show interest in them and hearing what they have to say. It's smart to break up provocative questions into multiple parts:

"So, what do you think about . . . ?"

"Seriously . . ."

"How funny is it when . . . ?"

While she types, if she is quickly distracted by a question that provokes her to respond, it will likely distract her from whatever she was writing. If the question is broken up into multiple parts and she notices continual IMs, she may delete what she was writing to respond to you, which allows you to direct the flow of dialog and create a distraction. If she responds to your distraction question, and you successfully changed the subject, then you've just directed dialog. You can concentrate on her positive characteristics and why you're interested. Thereafter, you can transition toward how much fun it would be to "meet up at some point." Don't ask, just suggest. Then, go for the phone number.

Chapter 9

Real-Time Speaking Tips:
Communicating on the Phone

The phone date can be far more difficult to approach than IM. With IM, she can only read what you write. On the phone, she hears you. That is why I stress over and over to be honest and be yourself with IM. If you are yourself via IM, you can be yourself—with nothing to fear—on the phone. You *must* be consistent. Any inconsistencies will be noticed and will eliminate your chance to seem genuine, which is your only chance to get a date based on good and honest context.

Remember, this book is not intended to teach you how to become an e-player, it is intended as a guide to present yourself, both personably and charismatically, to find a relationship. Be yourself and be as interesting as possible.

Study

Keep in mind your phone date is an opportunity, just as is the IM date. My advice is to save your IM conversation and read it over before making your phone call. It's important to remember as many details about the girl as possible. Being prepared will help reinforce the context you created in your IM conversation. Don't feel like you're cheating by saving the conversation; if you're interested enough to make the phone call, it's only logical to review the details you've already learned. Just make sure it isn't prohibited in the dating site's terms of use before doing it. I don't advise you tell her that you saved and reviewed the conversation because it could sound desperate and creepy. You're just being resourceful, and it's nobody's business but yours.

Visualize

Before you make your phone call, try to imagine a movie character with whom you feel a connection, one whose charisma and confidence you admire. Think about how he would approach the phone call—relaxed and smooth. Be yourself, but try to embrace the confidence and charisma that you admire and make it your own.

Practice

Play around with the tone of your voice prior to the call. Concentrate on your delivery. And remember to speak at a moderate pace and enunciate your words clearly. A speedy talker generally does not emanate confidence. Intensity on the phone is generally not a good idea. Vary your phraseology:

- "So, I know this is a non-sequitur, but it's interesting how . . . right?

- "Feels like there's definitely . . . it's hard to deny . . . ?"
- "Cassandra, ever feel like . . . ?

Laugh

Sorry, no examples—I can't teach you how to laugh, and I can't teach you when to laugh. In the spirit of what I've mentioned many times, be genuine. Laugh if she says something funny. Laugh if you say something really funny, but don't entertain yourself. Don't laugh harder than she laughs at your jokes.

Change

When chatting via IM, writing "lol" or "haha" is often an involuntary response. Often, we will respond with "haha" or "lol" just because we couldn't think of a better response. It could be funny and thought provoking to respond with, "Really? Did you actually laugh out loud, or did it just seem like a good response? :)"

Be Confident

When using IM, try to get her to focus on you and maintain her attention by constantly engaging her in the conversation. On the phone, her focus is already on you, and you have her attention, so you need to *be* confident, not just *act* confident.

Energy

You are expected to express more energy in the beginning of the conversation, but it needs to be reciprocated.

Unfortunately, if you are the person who initiates the call, until she exerts genuine energy, the pressure is on you to lead the conversation and fill in silences to reestablish and maintain balance. Once she begins enthusiastically asking you questions, it will no longer be your responsibility to fill in the silences.

Balance

Balance is established the same way on the phone as it is via IM; however, the phone begins with solid balance. Further, by discussing the topics and details that energized your IM conversation, you can re-establish the energy.

Don't

There is no right way to be interesting and smooth on the phone. There is, however, a wrong way. If you sound disinterested and overly nervous, you will likely bore her. A lack of enthusiasm and energy on a first phone call demonstrates a lack of confidence. Find a comfortable way to express your words with enthusiasm and energy.

Delivery

As mentioned earlier, enthusiasm and energy are contagious; they are even more so on the phone. Energy and enthusiasm are not based on speed, they're based on delivery. Don't rush your words. If you speak a bit slower, it will give her more opportunities to interrupt you with questions and discussion topics.

Compliments

Compliments can be more powerful on the phone because she can hear your enthusiasm and energy. When giving compliments on the phone, they can be effectively delivered as random comments or interruptions. For example: "By the way, you have an adorable voice. It matches up well with your smile." If you compliment with energy and enthusiasm, it's easier to make her blush on the phone because she can hear your energy.

Suggest

After a compliment is often the best time to follow up with a suggested meeting. For example, "It would be fun to grab a drink after work some time this week." Don't ask. Suggest. Then wait for her response. If she doesn't respond to an indirect question within four to five seconds, you can make a quick follow-up with "Oh, by the way . . . that was more of a question." She should respond to that.

Chapter 10

Real Conversation:
The Real Date

Once you've established a strong balance via IM, there are only two additional forms of communication to progress the rapport: a phone date and an in-person date. The energy from your IM will not last very long: a few days, maybe a week at most. When you transition to your first in-person date, remember that consistency in your behavior is key to a successful date.

Ideally, you should set a follow-up, real date quickly, but you don't want to go out with just any girl, so choose wisely. My strategies are meant to help build a connection between people who are compatible. If you aren't compatible, my techniques will likely not be as effective.

In person, present your personality in the same manner you did via IM, e-mail and, if applicable, on the phone. Consistent behavior will allow you to reestablish the energy from your preceding communications. Ask questions in the same way; compliment her in the same way. Discuss topics as a mechanism to create context just as you can in other communications.

Suggestions for Your In-person Date

- Always make eye contact when asking a question.
- When you greet her, stand if you're seated and address her by her first name, which is a great way to make someone feel more comfortable with you, as if you know them better (if you feel comfortable, go in for a casual, introductory hug). It helps further personalize the communication.
- Address her by her first name occasionally throughout the date.
- Smile, but don't force your smile. There's nothing worse than a fake smile. It's awkward and about as counterproductive as a burp. As mentioned previously, genuine energy and enthusiasm are contagious.
- Express interest; it will reinforce the other person's interest.
- Ask questions, but don't interrogate. Your goal is to reveal details through conversation, which will help you create additional context. For example, if you know what your date's favorite flower or color is, you can point them out if the opportunity presents itself. You can even go in a store and buy one during the date. Every detail you know about someone can serve as an opportunity to strengthen a personal connection. Another example: Do you know what her favorite style of art is? Take her to a museum

where she will be intrigued by a particular exhibit.

- Avoid intense behavior, drunken stupidity or being drugged up—try not to act out of character, and don't be creepy.

- You can work out before a date. If you schedule a date during the week after work, give yourself 45 minutes to go to the gym: Run, lift weights, burn off some energy and get your blood pumping. You will be more relaxed, yet it will energize you by releasing endorphins.

- Don't be physically aggressive. Remember, this is a first date, so she won't necessarily know when you're joking. It may make her uncomfortable if you're physically aggressive.

- Be a gentleman. Hold the door open. Show respect. Have class. Don't plan to invite her to your apartment on your first date; just let things happen naturally.

- Try not to reveal many vulnerabilities on the first date; mystery is exciting. Don't let your date figure you out that quickly. Even if she says, "I tend to wear my heart on my sleeve," show some self-restraint. It should take time to get to know someone. Showcase your most appealing characteristics on the first few dates so she's intrigued enough to continue getting to know you. While your date is not being filmed, remember that she is likely going to share every detail she remembers with her friends and possibly her family, so try not to give her anything negative to say.

- Grooming habits and hygiene are imperative. Yes, guys and girls, it's really important. And, for those of you who are rolling your eyes, there are actually quite a few people for whom it isn't common sense. You might be really surprised by what is and isn't common practice. First of all, brush your teeth—all of them, and do it before any date. If you don't have floss, buy some and use it, as well as mouthwash. If you are someone who is new to flossing, brushing and mouthwash, you should do all three of them, in that order.

- If you have a date after work and you know you won't have a chance to stop by your home before the meet-up, then think ahead—bring your floss, toothbrush, toothpaste, mouthwash and hair-styling product(s) to work with you.

- It always makes a person feel special when their date shows up looking their best. Give them that sense. Get your hair styled. Looking sloppy is usually a major turnoff.

- Perfume or cologne by itself is not now, nor should it ever be, used as a substitute for deodorant. If you don't have deodorant, get some immediately. I do not recommend a scentless deodorant unless you have allergies to the scent. The purpose of deodorant is to keep you from offending.

The Golden Rule

Never *ask* for another date while you're still on your first, second or third date. Do not misunderstand this to mean you shouldn't demonstrate interest. One way or another, you should express interest and enthusiasm—if it's genuine. If you don't, she'll assume you're not interested, or worse, that you're playing games. As mentioned previously, this is a guide to find genuine companionship, so don't play games. On that note, despite other advice you may have been given, if you enjoy a date and are interested in the person, it can be counterproductive to wait beyond the day following your date to reconnect and express interest. In fact, feel free to do so that night, perhaps a few hours after the date has ended. Any time you waste could represent a missed opportunity

Maintaining an edge is a very effective way to intrigue someone and may likely yield initial success, but don't be evasive. As I mentioned earlier, try not to make yourself the focus of conversation.

Your level of interest shouldn't be a secret. If you're naturally outgoing, you may feel comfortable or capable of expressing interest verbally or physically. A suggestion to verbalize interest would be to say something directly, without intensity: "I like your company" or "I'm glad we met." Use your own words, not mine, because she's not dating me, she's dating you. A physical example could be to subtly put your hand on her knee while enthusiastically telling a story or making a joke. Maybe you like the smell of her perfume, so you ask which perfume she is wearing and lean in a bit . . . you then gently take her wrist, but the smell has worn off her wrist so you inch a bit closer to her neck. Don't be sleazy, but many women respect boldness.

The Caveat

Suggest another meeting. Saying, "I'm enjoying this . . . we should do this again," is not asking for another date, but it does suggest it. Understand that The Golden Rule is intended to prevent you from seeming desperate. While you cannot control someone else's response, you are in control of what you say. Asking or saying something pushy, such as, "I want to see you again, which day next week works?" applies pressure and may yield unfavorable results. As I have said many times, *suggesting* a follow-up date and showing interest is strongly advised.

Epilogue

You and I may be very different, so I do not suggest you attempt to mimic my personality. As I've said over and over, being genuine is the best way to go, so don't be generic. Understand the theories I have explained and adapt them to your personality. Again, my goal is to help you achieve success in your quest to find companionship by being yourself.

Think of yourself as a rough gem that needs to be polished. You are not being dishonest by following advice; you are utilizing available resources and being pragmatic. As I've often written, dating is an interviewing process. You have competition. Do not be discouraged if someone ends an IM conversation unexpectedly or doesn't give you a phone number, because it is a game of numbers. If you put yourself out there often enough, you will improve your odds of success.

Appendix A

Abbreviations and Emoticons

Abbreviations

2moro — tomorrow

420 — marijuana

4eva — forever

abt — about

afc — average frustrated chump

AIM — AOL's Instant Messenger

amog — alpha male of the group

b4 — before

b4n — bye for now

bc — because

bcnu — be seeing you

bfaaf — best friends always and forever

bff — best friends forever

brb — be right back

bs — bullshit

btw — by the way

cya — cover your ass/See you

fb — fuck buddy or Facebook (more than likely, Facebook)

fml — fuck my life

gg or g/g or g2g — gotta go/got to go

gr8 — great

hs — high school

idky — I don't know why

im — instant message

ioi — indicator of interest

jk — just kidding

k — okay

l8r — later

lmao — laughing my ass off

lmfao — laughing my fucking ass off

lol — laugh out loud

nbd — no big deal

neg — a backhanded compliment

nm — not much

oic — oh, I see

olp — online player(s)

POF — Plenty of Fish

pov — point of view

pua — pickup artist

rotf — rolling on the floor (laughing)

sn — screen name (AIM/IM)

sol — shit out of luck

sp — spelling

thx — thanks

tmi — too much information

ttyl — talk to you later

ttys — talk to you soon

ty — thank you

tyvm — thank you very much

un — user name (AIM/IM)

wc or w/c — which

wtf — what the fuck

xoxo — hugs and kisses

Emoticons

An emoticon is a keyboard-produced or digitized graphic icon that represents emotional/facial expressions. Some commonly used keyboard emoticons include:

:-D (colon, hyphen, capital D) or **:D** (colon, capital D) = a big smiley face

:* (colon, asterisk) or **:-*** (colon, hyphen, asterisk) = kissy face

:/ (colon, forward slash) or **:-/** (colon, hyphen, forward slash) = sad face

:) (colon, close parenthesis) or **:-)** (colon, hyphen, close parenthesis) = smiley face

:P (colon, capital P) or **:-P** (colon, hyphen, capital P) = sticking out tongue playfully

;) (semi-colon, close parentheses) or **;-)** (semi-colon, hyphen, close parenthesis) = winky face

For a more extensive list of up-to-date emoticons, please refer to netlingo.com/smileys. Further, most dating websites' IM tool offers an array of graphically styled emoticons from which to choose.

Appendix B

Suggested Reading

Books

Act Like a Lady, Think Like a Man, Expanded Edition: What Men Really Think About Love, Relationships, Intimacy, and Commitment by Steve Harvey

The Art of Falling in Love: 4 Steps to Falling in Love, Staying in Love, Renewing Lost Love by Joe Beam

The Body Language of Dating: Read His Signals, Send Your Own, and Get the Guy by Tonya Reiman

The Conversation: How Men and Women Can Build Loving, Trusting Relationships by Hill Harper

Crash Course in Love by Steven Ward and JoAnn Ward

Crucial Conversations: Tools for Talking When Stakes Are High by Kerry Patterson, Joseph Grenny, Ron McMillan and Al Switzler

Data, A Love Story: How I Cracked the Online Dating Code to Meet My Match by Amy Webb

Essential Manners for Men, 2nd Edition: What to Do, When to Do It, and Why by Peter Post

The Female Brain by Louann Brizendine, M.D.

Fight Less, Love More: 5-Minute Conversations to Change Your Relationship without Blowing Up or Giving In by Laurie Puhn, J.D.

The Game: Penetrating the Secret Society of Pickup Artists by Neil Strauss

Get the Guy: Use the Secrets of the Male Mind to Find, Attract and Keep Your Ideal Man by Matthew Hussey

Have Him at Hello: Confessions from 1,000 Guys About What Makes Them Fall in Love . . . Or Never Call Back by Rachel Greenwald

I Love You, Let's Meet: Adventures in Online Dating by Virginia Vitzthum

The Illusion of Intimacy: Problems in the World of Online Dating by John C. Bridges

The Joy of Text: Mating, Dating, and Techno-Relating by Kristina Grish

Life Code: The New Rules for Winning in the Real World by Phil McGraw

Love at First Click: The Ultimate Guide to Online Dating by Laurie Davis

Love Online: A Practical Guide to Digital Dating by Phyllis Phlegar

May I Kiss You? A Candid Look at Dating, Communication, Respect, & Sexual Assault Awareness by Michael J. Domitrz

Men Are from Mars, Women Are from Venus: The Classic Guide to Understanding the Opposite Sex by John Gray

Modern Dating: A Field Guide by Chiara Atik

Saying What's Real: 7 Keys to Authentic Communication and Relationship Success by Ph.D. Susan Campbell

The Social Net: Understanding Our Online Behavior by Yair Amichai-Hamburger

Videos

When Strangers Click: Five Stories from the Internet directed by Robert Kenner

Additional Categories to Consider

Computers

Web/Social Networking

Web/General

Social Aspects/General

Social Aspects/Human-Computer Interaction

E-mail

Desktop Applications/E-mail

Computer Literacy

Personal Hygiene

Family and Relationships
Interpersonal Relations
Love and Romance
Romance
Sexuality

Health and Fitness
Beauty and Grooming
Men's Health
Sexuality
Women's Health

Humor
Adult
Relationships

Language Arts and Disciplines
General
Authorship
Communication Studies
Editing and Proofreading

Grammar and Punctuation

Linguistics

    Psycholinguistics

    Semantics

    Sociolinguistics

    Syntax

Spelling

Vocabulary

Philosophy

Language

Ethics and Moral Philosophy

Movements in

    Analytic

    Critical Theory

    Pragmatism

    Rationalism

Social/Psychology

Cognitive Psychology

Emotions

Social Psychology

Human Sexuality

Interpersonal Relations

Mental Health

Behaviorism

Anxieties and Phobias

Research and Methodology

Reference
Personal and Practice Guides
Etiquette
Writing Skills

Science
Energy
Philosophy and Social Aspects

Self-Help
General
Anxieties and Phobias
Motivational and Inspirational
Neuro-Linguistic Programming
Personal Growth
Self-Esteem
Success

Social Science
General
Anthropology
General
Cultural
Sociology

Technology and Engineering

Social Aspects

Telecommunications

Appendix C

Online Dating Sites

The following alphabetized list of online dating websites and brief descriptions is intended to serve as only a partial overview of the abundant options available. You may find that various online dating websites and services appeal to you, and you can test out any you find intriguing. Review options by using a search engine—there are plenty of those to choose from, too, such as Google, Yahoo, Dogpile and others. Of course, you can always ask a friend, or a friend of a friend, for a suggestion or recommendation, but it can't hurt to know what's available and decide what's best for you.

BlackPeopleMeet.com — An online dating community that specializes in connecting black singles in the United States.

Chemistry.com — A dating website that focuses on the process preceding the first date.

ChristianMingle.com — An online dating community that focuses on connecting Christian singles.

Cupid.com — A dating website that focuses on the communication process.

Date.com — A 100% free online dating community.

DateHookUp.com — A 100% free online dating community.

DatingForParents.com — An online dating service that specializes in connecting single parents.

eHarmony.com — The first online dating service to use a scientific approach to match highly compatible singles.

HowAboutWe.com — An online dating website that focuses on the offline dating process.

JDate.com — An online dating community that specializes in connecting Jewish singles.

LavaLife.com — An online dating and personals service that offers an extensive product selection.

Match.com — A global online dating community of diversified singles.

MuddyMatches.com — A rural online dating website that connects single farmers, rural singles, equestrian singles and country friends.

MySingleFriend.com — A UK dating website, the premise of which is that every member is described by his/her friends.

OKCupid.com — A free online dating website that offers a math-based matching system.

OurTime.com — A dating website for mature (older) singles.

PlentyOfFish.com — A free online dating website.

Tinder.com — A dating app that connects mutually interested singles who are located nearby.

Zoosk.com — An online dating service that uses Behavioral Matchmaking technology (based on personal browsing and clicking habits) to select matches for users.

There is a dating website for everyone, no matter what. Some additional, self-explanatory examples are:

STDSoulMates.com

CancerSurvivorDating.com

TransGenderDate.com

Appendix D

Punctuation for Social Communication

Comma = ,

Use a comma to space out your thoughts. For example: *"I think you're cute, fun to chat with, and I look forward to talking later."*

Period = .

Use a period to end a sentence. For example: *"I'm really glad we were able to connect."*

Double Hyphens = --

Double hyphens can be used to connect thoughts. For example: *"It's great to finally have a chance to relax--what an exhausting week."* In fact, a double hyphen can often be used interchangeably with a semicolon (;), although you may find that other people use it differently. However you choose to use punctuation, do so consistently to help demonstrate command of your language.

Question Mark = ?

Use a question mark to specify that a question is, in fact, a question. For example: *"What's your favorite type of food?"*

Exclamation Point = !

Use an exclamation point if you want to express loud emphasis. For example, if someone asks you if you're excited to learn that you've just won the lottery, feel free to respond, "Yes!" I'm not a big fan of using exclamation points because they are commonly interpreted as yelling.

Ellipses = . . .

You can use ellipses (generally, three consecutive periods) to indicate a pause in dialog. For example: *There's something special about you . . . your smile, your energy, the charismatic undertone of your profile."*

Quotation Marks = " "

Use quotations to specify words used, verbatim, in context. For example:

In your profile, you wrote: *"I can be feisty at times." When was the last time you found yourself being feisty?*

Acknowledgments

My parents, Arlene and Les Grafman, set an example of unconditional love and loyalty that fueled me to find companionship and happiness of my own. I always admired the way my parents would take care of one another when one was ill. They would hold hands when they walked together and would always support one another in making important decisions.

My parents never stopped believing in me and encouraged me every step of the way as I queried literary agents and publishers, worldwide. I'd like to thank my late mother for knowing that I would eventually be offered a publishing deal, despite the obstacles an author faces in pursuing a contract with a debut book.

I am grateful to my brother, Jordan, who always told me the truth about things whether I asked for advice or not. When offered a contract, Jordan encouraged me to follow through and get published. My sister-in-law, Melissa, set the standard with my brother for what I have found and want to help others find: true happiness and companionship. It always makes me smile to see the way Jordan and Melissa complement one another.

My Aunt Sandi and Uncle Chuck Schneider, who were like a second set of parents, always believed I could do anything I was determined to accomplish. Jeff Schneider (Chuck and Sandi's son), my cousin, gave valuable initial feedback and encouragement after reading the rough draft of this book. My friend Paul Aviles encouraged me to help people, and if it hadn't been for his suggestion, I never would have written this book. Scott Moses is another incredible friend who always encouraged me to pursue my dreams; when I told him I was writing this book, he said there was no one better to get it done.

I would be remiss to not mention the Fiorito family: Vincent, Sue, Angela, Dana, Michele and Tricia. My extended family has surrounded me with support, and I have seen examples of marriages that have encouraged me to want to find the same in my future: my parents', Jordan and Melissa's, Chuck and Sandi Schneider's, and Vincent and Sue Fiorito's.

Rainbow Books, Inc. and its now-late publisher, Betty Wright, saw the potential in this book. I thank them for giving me the opportunity to help people find companionship through today's most popular companionship medium: online dating. Special thanks go to Betsy Lampe for all her hard work in putting the final, polishing touches on this book. I am grateful that you are such a pleasure to work with.

About the Author

Keith Grafman grew up in the country on the outskirts of New York. He began his online dating ventures while attending Dickinson College. He graduated with a bachelor's degree in international business and management.

During college, Keith found that he had a knack for combining quick-witted communication skills with psychological strategy. What started as an exciting quest for companionship led to more than nine years of trial-and-error analysis to master the art of personality-projection marketing and online dating communications.

Over the years, Keith has encouraged many men and women to search for companionship online. He helps his clients create successful online dating profiles and teaches them to communicate effectively, with confidence.

Keith's online dating pursuit led to his getting married—a relationship that began with a string of e-mails.

For more information regarding Keith Grafman's seminars, public presentations or private consultations, please contact him at:

AdviceForDaters.com